At the first modern Olympics, held in Athens in 1896, heavyweight wrestler Carl Schuhmann (left) of Germany defeated Greece's Giorgios Tsitas to take the gold medal. A proud and honorable tradition had begun...

ABOUT THE AUTHORS

JAMIE MOFFATT has written four other books: *A Turning Point* (with Roger Olesen); *Wrestlers at the Trials*; *Strobel: Stories From A Life With Wrestling*; and *Adam Frey: A Collection of Blogs and Stories.*

The *Amateur Wrestling News* selected Jamie as the 2010 Bob Dellinger Award winner, naming him The National Wrestling Writer of the Year.

He is a graduate of Cornell University and is currently the Chairman of the EIWA Hall of Fame Committee. Jamie retired after a long professional career as a Management Consulting Partner with PricewaterhouseCoopers in 2000 and resides with his wife Betty in Cape May, NJ.

CRAIG SESKER has been the Communications Manager for USA Wrestling since 2006 and is the editor of USA Wrestling's member magazine, *USA Wrestler*, which has a circulation of more than 150,000. Sesker is a two-time National Wrestling Writer of the Year and won four National Associated Press Sports Editors writing awards during his career as a sportswriter.

This is Sesker's third book. He's the author of *Bobby Douglas: Life and Legacy of an American Wrestling Legend;* and *Driven to Excellence.*

Sesker resides in Colorado Springs, Colorado.

SAVING WRESTLING

**THE INSIDE STORY OF
THE SPORT'S EPIC FIGHT
TO STAY IN THE OLYMPICS**

**JAMES V. MOFFATT
& CRAIG SESKER**

SAVING WRESTLING: The Inside Story of the
Sport's Epic Fight to Stay in the Olympics

Copyright © 2013 By James V. Moffatt and Craig Sesker

All rights reserved. This book, or parts thereof, may not be reproduced in any form without permission from the publisher.

Published by Exit Zero Publishing
www.exitzero.us

Book and cover design by Jack Wright

Cover photo credits: Jordan Burroughs and Billy Baldwin
by Tony Rotundo/WrestlersAreWarriors
Helen Maroulis by John Sachs
Nenad Lalovic by AP Photo/Petros Giannakouris

First edition: October 2013

ISBN 978-0-9860523-0-9

CONTENTS

Ch 1 **Blindsided** P6

Ch 2 **Lausanne... Vote #1** P12

Ch 3 **Off the Whistle** P18

Ch 4 **Why Wrestling?** P22

Ch 5 **Phuket... The FILA Vote** P30

Ch 6 **Meet Nenad Lalovic** P34

Ch 7 **Tehran... A Perfect Storm** P38

Ch 8 **Building the Team** P46

Ch 9 **Meet the Press** P54

Ch 10 **Spreading the Good News** P58

Ch 11 **Fighting on Two Fronts** P62

Ch 12 **Modernizing the Sport** P72

Ch 13 **Love Letters** P80

Ch 14 **New York, New York** P84

Ch 15 **Moscow... A Turning Point** P94

Ch 16 **Los Angeles... Without the Iranians** P100

Ch 17 **St. Petersburg... Vote #2** P108

Ch 18 **Enter Phase Two** P120

Ch 19 **6-6-6** P130

Ch 20 **The New Rules** P138

Ch 21 **Fargo Dreams** P148

Ch 22 **Olympia's Hallowed Grounds** P156

Ch 23 **The Dog Days of Summer** P164

Ch 24 **Buenos Aires... Vote #3** P174

CHAPTER 1 / **Blindsided**

"I find it sadly ironic that the announcement that the IOC has recommended dropping wrestling as an Olympic sport occurred on the birthday of Abraham Lincoln, one of the 13 U.S. Presidents who wrestled." – Sandy Stevens, "The Voice of Wrestling"

DAN GABLE said he experienced an assortment of emotions when he first heard the news about the International Olympic Committee (IOC) Executive Board's recommendation to eliminate wrestling as a core Olympic sport. In Iowa City, Gable was lying in bed at 6 o'clock that February morning when he received word of the IOC decision. His wife, Kathy, was up early and on her computer. She walked into the bedroom and said, "I'm not sure if it's true, but I think they took wrestling out of the Olympics."

"It's probably nothing," Gable responded, "just a crazy blog. Don't worry."

Seconds later, Gable *was* worried. He jumped out of bed and went to check for himself. He scanned the major wrestling websites. It was true.

Then Gable, one of the toughest men to ever step on a wrestling mat, broke down and started crying at his keyboard. "I was really emotional and upset, but I wasn't really mad," he said. "I was more hurt in the beginning than anything."

Once the shock of the initial decision started to wear off and there was a realization that wrestling *could* remain part of the Olympic program, Gable was ready to jump in and do what he does best. Win the fight. Preserve the status of the sport that was prominent in the Olympic program as far back as 708 B.C.

Rich Bender awoke early on the morning of February 12, just after 5am, to prepare for his work day as the Executive Director at USA Wrestling. He was about to head into the bathroom in his Colorado Springs home to take a shower when his

Dan Gable broke down when he first heard of the IOC recommendation. Larry Slater

wife approached.

"You need to get your phone," Michelle Bender said, her eyes widening. "It's blowing up right now."

Bender's cellular phone had been ringing and buzzing with a flood of calls, emails and text messages from people around the country. And from around the world. He immediately sensed something was wrong. Terribly wrong.

At the exact moment he scooped up his iPhone, a text message flashed across the screen. It was a message sent by Gable from his home.

"Worst possible decision," Gable's message read.

Bender was fully aware that the IOC Executive Board was voting in Switzerland that day to recommend that one core sport be removed from the Olympic Games program for 2020 so that a new sport could be added.

"The evening before, I had a conversation with the United States Olympic Committee about the process and the vote," Bender said. "I was given some pretty high-level assurance that wrestling wasn't going to be part of the discussion. I was told it was going to be modern pentathlon or taekwondo or field hockey. I went to bed that night not expecting to hear anything negative the next morning."

But that changed when he saw Gable's text message. Bender immediately sat down at his computer and quickly confirmed the unthinkable had happened.

"I obviously was surprised — it was absolutely stunning," Bender said. "I was so upset that I wanted to punch somebody in the mouth. My initial reaction was incredible pain, understanding what the sport means to the Olympics and to our organization. The Olympic designation provides a great deal of credibility to our sport in our country and around the world. I started getting really angry with our international federation [FILA] and individuals within that federation. I got really upset initially and then I quickly realized that doesn't do any good. I knew I had to put those feelings aside and focus on what I could do personally and what our country could do to keep our sport in the Olympics."

Like Gable and Bender, many people in the U.S. woke up to the shocking news before they even ate breakfast that day. Sandy Stevens, wrestling's iconic public address announcer who called matches during the 1984 and 1996 Games, remembered, "I was at home last February 12, listening to Chicago's new station, WBBM, when they announced the IOC's decision. I know I said an out-loud, 'What?!' I'm thinking I couldn't have heard this right.

"Immediately I checked themat.com and Facebook and found dozens of others, both in and out of our sport, expressing the same dismay, disbelief and shock that I felt. Also, non-wrestling friends soon began calling or emailing me; even they were stunned and offended by the decision. The immediate calls to action by those who love our sport gave (and give) me hope. But how horribly sad that politics, money and inept FILA leadership brought us to this point."

The IOC recommendation had been made in Europe, where it was already around lunchtime.

In Belgrade, Serbia, FILA Bureau member Nenad Lalovic was sitting in his office when he received a phone call from a friend who lives in Switzerland.

"My friend heard about it on the radio," said Lalovic, a successful businessman. "I checked on the internet and I was astonished. When we heard the news, the FILA members were not even aware there was a meeting in Lausanne [at the

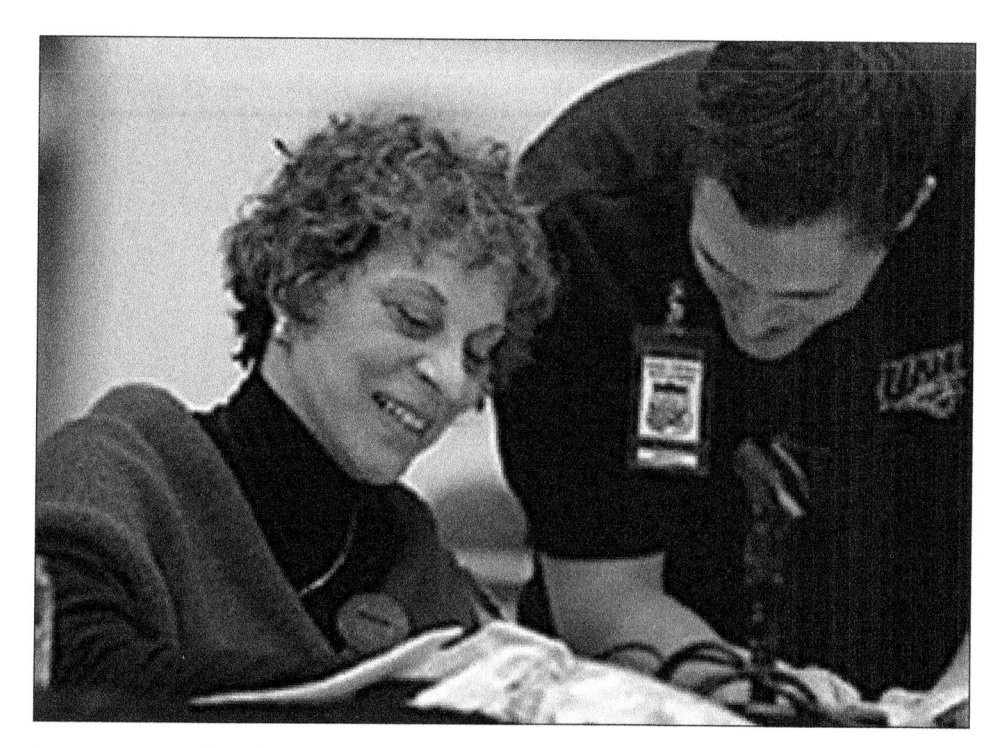

Even non-wrestling friends of Sandy Stevens were calling her in dismay with the vote to drop wrestling from the Olympics.

IOC headquarters]. The other sports had people in the office there, but nobody from FILA had information that such a vote was taking place. Never before was the president or general secretary of FILA telling us this. We asked many times if there would be some action about the Olympic program, but the leaders from FILA said you don't have to worry."

In Frankfurt, Germany, Olympic gold medalist Jordan Burroughs was sitting in the airport awaiting a flight. He was in a group with American freestyle teammates Tervel Dlagnev, Coleman Scott, Obe Blanc and Max Askren. They were on their way to the upcoming World Cup in Tehran, Iran. They watched on a small, overhead television as the news flashed across the screen on a BBC World News broadcast. The team's jovial, upbeat mood suddenly became somber and quiet as the athletes began looking at each other in disbelief.

"We saw the little blurb that wrestling was being dropped from the 2020 Olympics, and then they went to a commercial," Burroughs said. "We looked at each other like, this can't be real and this must be a joke. Then they came back from the commercial and started talking more about it. That's when it hit us that this was really happening."

Burroughs and his teammates were stuck in Germany with no internet connection and virtually no way to fully comprehend what was going on back in the U.S.

"I couldn't believe it," Burroughs said. "It was crazy and just surreal. I was angry, shocked, frustrated and confused. I felt betrayed and I felt a sense of sadness. We all were asking, 'What went wrong and what is happening?' We were all kind of freaking out."

In Lagos, Nigeria, Olympic gold medalist and national hero Daniel Igali's plane had just landed as he returned home. Television crews quickly descended upon Igali, a member of Nigeria's Parliament and the country's National freestyle coach, after spotting him in the airport.

"The TV reporters started asking me questions and wanted to get my reactions to wrestling not being a part of the 2020 Olympics," Igali said. "I thought it was some kind of April Fool's joke. I had no idea and no inkling this was coming. Never in my wildest dreams did I think that this would happen to one of the greatest sports in the world. I was shocked at first, and then I was angry."

In Herning, Denmark, Erik Nyblom was at work when he received a message from his country's Junior coach. Nyblom, Vice-President of the Denmark Wrestling Federation and father of World bronze medalist Hakan Nyblom, couldn't believe what he was hearing.

"I thought it wasn't real," he said. "I thought it was a sick rumor spread by somebody to justify some very big rules changes or trying to get rid of Greco-Roman wrestling or something crazy like that."

Nyblom quickly fired up his computer and checked the internet. "After finding a couple of stories confirming the news, at first I was frustrated and felt cheated," he said. "I thought this was going to be the end of our sport, or at least the beginning of the end."

In Honolulu, Hawaii 15-year-old Teshya Alo first heard the news of the IOC Executive Board's recommendation about wrestling while clicking on USA Wrestling's website, themat.com, while she was at school. Alo is a two-time women's Cadet national champion with dreams of competing for the U.S. in future Olympic Games.

"I was very sad at first, and very surprised," Alo said. "I didn't think it was real at first. Wrestling was one of the first Olympic sports. I started feeling better when I heard there was an opportunity the sport could be saved and kept in the Olympics."

USA Wrestling Vice-President Greg Strobel woke up in Bethlehem, Pennsylvania to a 6am text message — the IOC had done their 'dirty deed'. Their Executive Board voted against wrestling. Strobel didn't understand.

"The previous evening I was on the conference call of USA Wrestling officers. Towards the end of the call, Bender mentioned that the IOC Board meeting was taking place and that he had been told that 'wrestling was safe'. As we hung up around 9:30pm I had the feeling all was A-OK."

Obviously it was pretty far from A-OK.

CHAPTER 2 / **Lausanne... Vote #1**

AT 9AM on February 12, 2013 the 15 members of the International Olympic Committee (IOC) Executive Board gathered around a conference table at the prestigious Lausanne Palace hotel in the IOC headquarter city of Lausanne, Switzerland. The schedule called for the 12 men and three women to receive reports from several IOC Commissions, along with updates on the activities of the IOC administration and to make preparations for future editions of the Olympic Games.

Most importantly, during the morning session they had to vote to eliminate one existing core sport from the Olympics starting in 2020 so that a new sport could be added to those Games. The Executive Board's decision would be in the form of a recommendation; the full IOC membership (the General Assembly) would have to ratify that recommendation in a vote later in the year.

IOC President, Count Jacques Rogge, conducted the meeting. Rogge was completing his 12th and final year at the helm (Rogge was a three-time Olympian in rowing for his native Belgium) of the IOC. Early in Rogge's term, back in 2002, he led the initiative to control the size, cost and complexity of the Games. He capped the Olympic Programme at 28 sports. In 2007, the concept of 25 core sports and three additional 'provisional' sports was adopted. If the IOC, in their quest to 'modernize' the Games, wanted to bring a new sport onboard, an existing sport would have to be dropped. Thus, the February 12 vote.

Rogge could feel comfortable with the Executive Board, since half of the members were practically neighbors, hailing from various Western European countries. The geographical makeup of the other half of the Board was scattered — one from Australia, one from Eastern Europe, two from the Far East, two

IOC leader Jacques Rogge presided over the Executive Board vote to eliminate wrestling from the Olympic Games.

from Africa, and remarkably, just one member from the American hemisphere (Guatemala).

Among the first orders of business scheduled for the group was the delivery of a report by the Olympic Programme Commission. According to the IOC website, 'the Programme Commission is responsible for reviewing and analysing the programme of sports, disciplines and events, as well as the number of athletes in each sport.'

In an effort to ensure the Olympic Games remain relevant to sports fans of all generations, the Olympic Programme Commission systematically reviews every sport following each edition of the Games.

After the 2012 Games in London, the Commission analyzed each sport against 39 criteria, including television ratings, ticket sales, anti-doping policy, global participation and popularity. However, there were no official rankings or recommendations contained in the report. *

After reviewing the Programme Commission evaluation report, it was time for the group to vote on dropping one of the 26 core sports. Five sports were on the ballot — canoeing, field hockey, modern pentathlon, taekwondo and wrestling.

Reportedly, senior international federation officials from four of the five sports on the ballot were visiting in Lausanne at the time of the meeting. It was customary that sporting officials could be found in the hotel lobby, restaurants and bars the night before any significant IOC vote. Wrestling was the only sport without a representative in attendance — a strategic error, no doubt, on the part of wrestling's leadership.

By IOC procedure, each Executive Board member had one vote, cast by secret ballot. The sport to be dropped needed to receive a majority — eight — of the votes. President Rogge abstained from the vote, leaving 14 members to select the doomed sport.

In the first round of secret-ballot votes, five members voted for wrestling and five members voted for modern pentathlon. Field hockey received two votes, with one each for canoeing and taekwondo. It looked like it would come down to wrestling or modern pentathlon as the sport facing elimination.

Since no sport received a majority of the votes, the members voted again. In the second round, two members changed their vote, moving wrestling to the brink. The tallies were: wrestling 7; modern pentathlon 4; canoeing 1; field hockey 1; and taekwondo 1.

---

* To read all 39 IOC evaluation criteria, visit: http://www.olympic.org/Documents/Commissions_PDFfiles/Programme_commission/2012-06-28-IOC-evaluation-criteria-for-sports-and-disciplines.pdf

An unanswered question — why did two voters change their minds at this point to eliminate wrestling?

The IOC voting procedures now called for a tie-breaking round among the three third-place sports. Whichever sport received the lowest number of votes would be taken out of consideration for elimination. Canoeing received the least number of votes — three — and was now safe.

The next round of voting among the four 'finalists' produced a strange quirk. While wrestling received the most elimination votes — six — that was one less vote than they received in round two. That could be perceived as a positive sign for the sport, especially since modern pentathlon received five votes, one *more* than they had in round two. An Executive Board member was presumably changing his/her mind between wrestling and modern pentathlon. Field hockey came away with just three votes and taekwondo was looking particularly safe, receiving nary a vote.

Only the IOC Board members know why and what happened next — round five, the final round of the vote.

Two members apparently switched their vote from modern pentathlon to wrestling...

Wrestling – 8 votes
Field hockey – 3 votes
Modern pentathlon – 3 votes

By virtue of these eight votes the IOC Executive Board recommended that one of the original Olympic sports, wrestling, be sent packing from the Games.

As America woke up on this February morning, at a pre-scheduled noon press conference in Lausanne, IOC spokesman Mark Adams announced the verdict — a virtual death penalty on the sport of wrestling. He let the world know that the IOC Executive Board had voted to recommend to the full IOC General Assembly that wrestling would no longer be a core Olympic sport after the 2016 Games.

Adams' summing-up included this comment, "This is a process of renewing and renovating the program for the Olympics. In the view of the Executive Board, this was the best program for the Olympic Games in 2020. It's not a case of what's wrong with wrestling; it is what's right with the 25 core sports."

But he added an escape clause, "Today's decision is not final. The session [the IOC general assembly meeting scheduled for September 8 in Argentina] is sovereign and the session will make the final decision."

In the coming months wrestling would now compete with seven other sports to try to earn its way back onto the Olympic program as a 'provisional' sport in

2020 and 2024. The IOC Executive Board would meet in late May in St. Petersburg, Russia to hear presentations from the eight sports eligible for consideration as the new sport — baseball/softball, karate, roller sports, sport climbing, squash, wakeboarding, wrestling and wushu. After the presentations, the Executive Board would vote to designate one to four of those sports onto a shortlist; then, during their scheduled meeting in Buenos Aires in September, the full 103-person IOC general assembly would vote to add one as the new Olympic sport.

Yes, wrestling was given a virtual death sentence, but it was not quite dead, yet.

The IOC Executive Board

President	NATION	SPORT
Count Jacques Rogge	Belgium	Rowing*
Vice-Presidents		
Mr Thomas Bach	Germany	Fencing*
Ms Nawal El Moutawakel	Morocco	Track*
Mr Ser Miang Ng	Singapore	Sailing
Sir Craig Reedie	Great Britain	Badminton
Members		
Dr René Fasel	Switzerland	Ice Hockey
Mr Sam Ramsamy	South Africa	Swimming
Mr Patrick Joseph Hickey	Ireland	Judo
Mrs Gunilla Lindberg	Sweden	Bobsled, Luge
Mr John D. Coates	Australia	Rowing
Mr Juan Antonio Samaranch Jr	Spain	Modern Pentathlon
Mr Sergey Bubka	Ukraine	Track*
Mrs Claudia Bokel	Germany	Fencing*
Mr Ching-Kuo Wu	China	Boxing
Mr Willi Kaltschmitt Luján	Guatemala	Baseball, Boxing

* Denotes Olympian

CHAPTER 3 / Off the Whistle

THE DAY the IOC recommendation came down, Rich Bender thought back to a conversation he had with then-FILA President Raphael (Raphy) Martinetti during the 2012 Olympic Games in London, England. "Martinetti assured me that wrestling was going to stay on the core list of Olympic sports," Bender said. "He obviously either wasn't telling me the truth or he didn't know. It was probably a little bit of both. If we had any idea wrestling was in any danger, we obviously would've done everything we could to keep that from happening."

Bender also thought back to a conversation he had with Chicago businessman Bill Scherr, a past World champion and Olympic medalist, in 2009. Scherr had led the Chicago bid to try and land the 2016 Olympics.

"Bill and I had talked about wrestling's reputation with the International Olympic Committee, and how it wasn't good and how wrestling wasn't perceived positively by members of the IOC," Bender said. "I arranged a meeting and Bill flew to Herning, Denmark for the World Championships in 2009. Bill and I met with Martinetti and we gave him some of the information that Bill had received from the IOC. Martinetti assured us that it was not the case. He said wrestling had strong relationships with the IOC and was a firm partner with the IOC and the Olympics.

"However, there certainly was some indication that wrestling wasn't perceived positively by the IOC. If you translate that to say there was a possibility wrestling would be kicked off the program, you can interpret that however you want. I think that would be pretty extreme and a pretty big assumption to think that."

Shortly after Bender heard the bad news, he drove to USA Wrestling headquarters in Colorado Springs to meet with his Communications Director, Gary

Abbott. After speaking with USA Wrestling President Jim Ravannack and bringing him into the loop, Bender and Abbott drove downtown to meet with USOC Chief Executive Officer Scott Blackmun.

"I wanted to find out exactly what the IOC had done," Bender said. "Was this a final decision? When I found out it wasn't, my next thought was — what can we do to change this decision? We had to learn the process and we had to develop a game plan for what we wanted to do. This was a recommendation and not a final decision. We had to act quickly and figure out a way to do everything we could to keep wrestling in the Olympic Games."

Back in his office, Bender placed a phone call to Martinetti. "How could this possibly happen?" Bender asked Martinetti early that morning.

"It's impossible for them to take wrestling out of the Olympics," Martinetti fired back. "They can't do that."

Following a short conversation with Martinetti, Bender made phone calls to Stan Dziedzic, who was in Thailand, and former Olympic wrestlers Jim and Bill Scherr. Bender, Dziedzic and the Scherrs all strongly agreed on one issue in particular — Martinetti was a big part of the problem with the IOC.

After those discussions, Bender placed a second phone call to Martinetti. He got right to the point. "Based on the information I've seen," Bender told the FILA President, "I think it's necessary for you to resign."

"That's impossible," Martinetti responded tersely. "You need to call your IOC members and ask them to tell [IOC President Jacques] Rogge to change the decision."

"I'm unaware of that being a process that's available," Bender said.

Bender was right. The IOC President did *not* have the power to randomly change the decision of the IOC Executive Board. But Bender and top U.S. officials were determined to see one change take effect — the leadership of FILA.

All of wrestling's greatest names around the country were receiving dozens of phone calls and emails from the media, asking for reactions from those on the front line. The 2004 Olympic gold medalist Cael Sanderson, who has coached Penn State to three NCAA titles after winning four of his own for Iowa State, was among those who jumped in right away to defend wrestling's place in the Olympic Games.

"The Olympics are every wrestler's dream," Sanderson said in an interview on February 12. "It's like the World Cup of soccer. It's the most prestigious and premier event we have. It's the very top of the pyramid. It's the Super Bowl. Just the thought is definitely a tragedy. But I think wrestling is very strong worldwide, and we're going to find out just how strong."

Greg Strobel recalls the beginning of the journey to save Olympic wrestling,

"I was not optimistic about wrestling's chances to make a comeback right away. To do so, the IOC Board in just three months' time would have to reverse their earlier decision. That would not be an easy or natural thing for them to do. Yet, the wrestling leaders in the U.S. were ready to give it their best shot. USA Wrestling was ready to put its full energy and resources behind this."

"I was part of an emergency conference call that Tuesday morning at 11am," said Strobel. "The group of us from USA Wrestling and a couple of other leaders from the sport shared what information we knew and went right to work. By mid-afternoon we had put together a series of talking points for the public and spokespeople to follow. We were off and running."

The battle to keep wrestling in the Olympics was underway.

TALKING POINTS ABOUT WRESTLING AND THE OLYMPICS
By USA Wrestling
02/12/2013
USA Wrestling has created these talking points for those in the wrestling community in our nation who may be speaking about our sport in light of today's International Olympic Committee announcement (to eliminate wrestling from Olympic Games). Please read them carefully and refer to them in your public statements.

1) FILA, the international wrestling federation, the U.S. Olympic Committee and USA Wrestling did not expect this announcement. None of these leadership groups anticipated that wrestling was being considered for this.

2) This is a decision by the International Olympic Committee Executive Board. The recommendation is that wrestling not be included as a core sport at the 2020 Olympic Committee. This is not a final decision.

3) The next step is for the IOC Executive Board to recommend a sport for the final spot in the 2020 Olympics. Wrestling will be considered for the position along with seven other sports, which happens in May in St. Petersburg, Russia. Then, the next step is for the entire International Olympic Committee to vote on the final program for the 2020 Olympics, which occurs in September in Buenos Aires, Argentina.

4) This is an opportunity for wrestling to tell its story, not only to the International Olympic Committee leadership but also to the entire world.

5) Wrestling is one of the original sports in the ancient Olympic Games in Greece. Wrestling was also included in the first modern Olympic Games in 1896.

6) Wrestling is one of the most diverse sports in the world, with nearly 200 nations from all continents participating in the sport.

OFF THE WHISTLE   21

Key leaders in America's drive to save Olympic wrestling were Rich Bender and Gary Abbott of USA Wrestling and Jim Scherr, a former Executive Director of USA Wrestling and past CEO of the USOC.

7) Wrestling is an inclusive sport which provides opportunities worldwide, regardless of geography, race, gender or physical characteristics. Anybody can wrestle.

8) Among Olympic sports, wrestling has more variety of nations which win Olympic medals than almost every other sport. Wrestling is popular all around the world, and many nations have successful athletes and programs in the sport.

9) This is a challenge for the entire wrestling community on the world level. USA Wrestling, as the national governing body in the United States, is putting its full energy and resources behind this. We will work with our wrestling brothers and sisters everywhere on earth to maintain our sport on the Olympic program.

10) Wrestlers are known for their work ethic. As a community, we will work tirelessly from this point forward letting the world know about why wrestling is so special. We believe that we have the ability to be successful.

11) Be honest. Explain why wrestling is so important to you, and also important to the world. Do not be negative or critical of the IOC. It is our job to make them our supporters and allies moving forward.

12) USA Wrestling's Executive Committee, Board of Directors, staff and leaders are already involved working on this issue. We will continue to update the wrestling community about what is going on.

13) What can you do right now? Stay informed. Join "Keep Wrestling In the Olympics" Facebook page, which can be found at Keep Wrestling in the Olympics.

CHAPTER 4 / **Why Wrestling?**

WHEN THE IOC announced that their Executive Board voted by secret ballot to recommend eliminating wrestling as an Olympic sport, an obvious question was, 'Why wrestling? Why not one of the other sports?' The IOC did not publically answer those questions to everyone's satisfaction.

Many people, both inside and outside the international wrestling community, were not only asking the question, but were attempting to find a reasonable answer to an unreasonable turn of events. Most fingers pointed in one of two directions...

1. The IOC, in particular the Executive Board;
2. International wrestling's governing body, FILA (Fédération Internationale des Luttes Associées; International Federation of Associated Wrestling Styles), in particular President Raphy Martinetti.

Not surprisingly, most of the criticism of the IOC did not come from the wrestling world. FILA and wrestling federation leaders globally knew that their only chance for survival lay in the hands of the IOC voters who could potentially reverse the disastrous recommendation in the coming months. There was no sense in calling them out — in fact FILA would later go back to the IOC Executive Board on bended knee. It was left to the columnists and bloggers to point out that politics, cronyism and conflicts of interest surrounded the actions of the Executive Board.

Guilty Party #1 — The IOC's Executive Board

For sure, wrestling was facing a stacked deck of IOC voters. Had there been a more geographically diverse group that would have included some representatives from wrestling-friendly countries such as the USA, Canada, Russia, Iran, India, Japan

Critics saw Juan Antonio Samaranch Jr. as having a potential conflict of interest when serving simultaneously as an IOC Executive Board member and Vice-President of modern pentathlon's International Federation.

or Korea, rather than the majority hailing from Western Europe, there likely would have been more sentiment for wrestling rather than, let's say, modern pentathlon or field hockey. Among the 14 countries represented on the IOC Executive Board, only Germany, Sweden and Ukraine have won Olympic medals in wrestling in the last 20 years. No one on the Board had the slightest connection with wrestling.

But there *was* a Board connection, a most important connection, with modern pentathlon — the sport that was widely anticipated to be the one eliminated. Juan Antonio Samaranch Jr. is Vice-President of the International Modern Pentathlon Union. He is also a member of the IOC Executive Board, casting his secret ballot vote while, some might acknowledge, lobbying fellow Board members. His legendary father presided over the IOC from 1980-2001. Many of the current Executive Board members were appointed as IOC members during the senior Samaranch's lengthy term in office.

Bill Dwyre, columnist for the *Los Angeles Times*, observed what many already knew: "According to International Softball Federation chief Don Porter, who was at the scene, modern pentathlon survived, barely. Wrestling did not. Porter is in Lausanne, Switzerland, because his sport of women's softball was cut from the Games before last summer's London Games and he is hoping to have it reinstated at meetings in May. So he goes wherever the IOC is and lobbies. Cocktail parties and coffee shops are his life."

"These are their Games," Porter says poignantly in the interview with Dwyre, "and we have to play them."

Dwyre continued, "Reports from Lausanne said that the wrestling federation didn't push as hard as the modern pentathlon people, that these are games won or lost not on the playing field, but standing alongside a bar, a glass of fine Bordeaux in hand. Reports also cited the importance of Juan Antonio Samaranch Jr., son of the former IOC president, on the side of modern pentathlon."

"There's a stench of something unsavory here," wrote Reid Redgrave on Fox Sports. "It feels like another politically motivated decision by the most political organization in sports."

Rich Bender was quoted in a *USA Today* article: "Tuesday's decision was made by 'uninformed individuals' who don't understand the sport's Olympic value." He also noted that neither the U.S. Olympic Committee nor any former wrestlers are represented on the 15-member IOC Executive Board.

Writing in the *Christian Science Monitor* on February 12, Mark Sappenfield said the IOC "is still struggling to outgrow its reputation as a cabal of out-of-touch elitists." He indicted the Executive Board of making a decision "that was so wildly wrong-headed that it exposes the movement to ridicule and allegations of foul play" and questioned why the IOC would keep taekwondo, "a sport widely seen as being insignificant outside South Korea, if not to appease Samsung, the South Korean technology company that is a major Games supporter."

Take a look at some statistics that were (or certainly should have been) known to the IOC voters...

• Wrestling is more popular than modern pentathlon by just about any measure. At the London Games, athletes from 71 countries competed in wrestling. Athletes from 26 countries competed in modern pentathlon. FILA boasts 177 member nations. Modern pentathlon's national federation has 108.

• Reportedly, wrestling generates nearly twice the TV audience worldwide than does modern pentathlon, both in terms of maximum (58.5 million vs. 33.5 million) and average (23 million vs. 12.5 million) viewership.

• Wrestling awards 72 Olympic medals; modern pentathlon awards six.

• Wrestling was a tough ticket to acquire in London. In fact, wrestling was sold out there... every seat, every day. Countless fans were unable to see the matches in person because tickets were already long gone. And this in Great Britain, a country

Wrestling leaders cited FILA President Raphy Martinetti's poor relationship with the IOC as a major contributor to the vote against wrestling.

that does not have much in the way of a following in wrestling.

Modern pentathlon has been on the brink of elimination from the Olympics before. In fact in 2002, the IOC Programme Commission recommended to the IOC Executive Board that they drop the sport from the Olympic Games. However, a major campaign to override that verdict was waged. As part of the campaign Klaus Schormann, president of the Union Internationale de Pentathlon Moderne (UIPM), wrote a compelling letter and made a personal visit with his executive team to newly inducted IOC President Jacques Rogge, offering a plethora of reasons why modern pentathlon should be saved. Also, HSH Prince Albert of Monaco addressed the IOC in Switzerland on behalf of the cause, reaffirming modern pentathlon as the soul of the Olympic movement, to be maintained for the sake of Olympic tradition and values. Prince Albert was the honorary president of the UIPM — and an IOC member.

Indeed, this sport is experienced in fighting off its back. You have to give today's modern pentathlon leaders credit for averting disaster once again — they lobbied the IOC Board members hard and often in support of their athletes. "We were considered weak in some of the scores in the Program Commission report but strong in others," Samaranch told the Associated Press. "We played our cards to the best of our ability and stressed the positives. Tradition is one of our strongest assets, but we are also a multi-sport discipline that produces very complete people."

The Associated Press reported that UIPM's Schormann again lobbied vigorously to protect his sport's Olympic status and it paid off in the end. "We have promised things and we have delivered," said Schormann after the IOC decision. "That gives me a great feeling. It also gives me new energy to develop our sport further and never give up."

When asked by Karolos Grohmann of Reuters whether his double capacity was a conflict of interest, Samaranch said: "I am here in my capacity as Executive Board member."

Guilty Party #2 — FILA and its President, Raphael Martinetti

If the other sports vying to get in — or stay in — the Olympics were guilty of heavy-duty lobbying of the IOC, well, the FILA leader for the last 11 years was guilty of taking the opposite approach. He couldn't, or wouldn't, develop any sort of positive relationship with the IOC Executive Board members.

Bob Condron, now-retired Director of Media Services for the U.S. Olympic Committee, recalls Martinetti's first meeting with IOC President Rogge. "About 10 years ago Martinetti invited Rogge and some IOC staff to come visit the new FILA headquarters that Martinetti had just purchased on behalf of FILA in Corsier-Sur Vevey. It was a humongous castle, named Rue du Chateau #6. It had a courtyard as big as a soccer field and went on and up from there. When Rogge saw it, he rolled his eyes. I'm sure he was thinking — and the IOC is subsidizing a place like this for you to work?"

The relationship between Martinetti and Rogge never took off — and actually deteriorated, according to people familiar with the situation.

FILA Board Vice-President Stan Dzeidzic says of Martinetti, "He had his problems. FILA was *his* organization. He couldn't communicate with the rest of the world. The membership didn't know just how bad a shape the organization really was in. He had a mole [FILA Board member Ahmet Ayik from Turkey] in all the meetings. Martinetti was not that smart, yet he was politically astute. He possessed good language skills and was a very competent wrestling official. But, the more we learned about Martinetti the more we saw power clouding his judgment."

One of the main charges against Martinetti was the extraordinarily poor quality of work in FILA's submission of the response to the IOC questionnaire that the organization sends to each Olympic sport authority every four years. Condron describes the response submitted by Martinetti and his staff last year as "an absolute non-effort. For instance, in the area where FILA was asked to describe its youth program, the response was something like, 'FILA has a Youth Program.' Martinetti was capable, but just too arrogant and antagonistic towards the IOC. He didn't feel that he needed to waste any of his time answering to the IOC — or anyone else for that matter."

Apparently, no one serving on FILA's 22-member Bureau or any executives at any of the national wrestling federations ever reviewed the response to this most important IOC document until *after* the crippling February vote. No one recognized until it was too late that the proper internal controls were never in place to prevent this kind of colossal management blunder.

Jim Scherr, who would soon join the FILA Bureau and play a significant role in the campaign to keep wrestling as an Olympic sport, offered his views on why Martinetti was able to stay in power for 11 years despite his obvious flaws: "It is just by nature very difficult to remove a sitting International Federation President. I am not sure why all the members of the Bureau tolerated him, but he essentially had, as the President, enough influence and power to have their tenure shortened and made miserable while he was there. Also, it sounds like the Bureau members did not do enough due diligence or ask enough questions to understand the real facts about what was happening at FILA," said Scherr.

Russian Olympic Committee President Alexander Zhukov echoed Condron's thoughts, saying that the questionnaire response was an "embarrassing" presentation by wrestling's world governing body and that it was to blame for the sport being cut from the Olympic program.

IOC Board member Sergei Bubka said that wrestling was dropped from the core Olympic program because the sport is run by a federation with deficient management and no clear rules on how to punish breaches of "ethical norms." He outlined the arguments made before the vote, saying that FILA lacked important governance structures. "As of today there's no commission for athletes, no administration for decisions of the federation's executive committee... there's no women's committee," he told a Russian correspondent.

The Russians were particularly vocal in blaming Martinetti for wrestling's fall. The Russian Amateur Wrestling Federation (FSBR) website www.wrestrus.ru stated: "The officials of FSBR claim that the problem mainly lies in the current FILA President and his very complicated relations with IOC."

The same website contained stories printed by the Russian newspaper *Vzgliad* on February 14, quoting numerous leaders of Russia's wrestling family. Russian IOC member Shamil Tarpishchev declared that the IOC was dissatisfied with the organization of work and activities in FILA, and this, in part, explained why wrestling had been recommended for exclusion.

"Yesterday's decision has nothing to do with politics, and it was not aimed specifically against our country or any other country. IOC has many complaints as to the organization of work and activities inside FILA. They have got lots of problems inside the federation," Tarpishchev noted.

"FILA has weak links with IOC, that's true," said Georgiy Bryusov, the first Vice-President of FSBR.

Russian Wrestling Federation leader Mikhail Mamiashvili acknowledged that FILA was part of the problem. "I believe that Martinetti's task was to work hard, socialize and defend wrestling's place before the IOC," said Mamiashvili in comments reported by the Itar-TASS news agency. "He has delivered catastrophic work and didn't defend our sport before the IOC."

In an interview with the Greek paper *Kathimerini*, Serbian FILA Bureau member Nenad Lalovic admitted, "The IOC is in charge of its events and it is quite natural that it should want all its events to be interesting to the spectatorship. We were not listening to these warnings. Worse, we, the board members, were not informed of that. In conclusion I would say that the recommendation by the IOC to leave wrestling out of the Olympics is mainly our fault, FILA's fault, not the IOC."

Several wrestling leaders from the USA also found fault with wrestling's leadership. Mike Novogratz, chairman of Beat-the Streets in New York City, says, "The IOC was very frustrated with FILA and its leadership, specifically Raphy Martinetti. I honestly think it was as simple as that."

In her May 8 story in the *Washington Post*, Liz Clarke reported that Bill Scherr said he wasn't surprised by the decision, having been warned by IOC insiders that wrestling was at risk. The major problem was that FILA didn't respond in earnest to a mandate that all Olympic sports raise more private money, modernize with an eye toward boosting TV coverage, leverage social media and develop gender equity.

Some observers also point to a scandal dating back to the 2008 Olympics in Beijing, when the IOC took a dim view of a wrestling incident. The Swedish Greco-Roman wrestler Ara Abrahamian disrupted the awards ceremony by discarding his bronze medal in protest of controversial calls by the judges that went against him in his semi-finals match. The IOC disqualified him and subsequently much discussion arose, not just about Abrahamian's behavior but also about the alleged practice of wrestling judges accepting bribes for many years.

Wade Schalles, a two-time NCAA champion, saw FILA, USA Wrestling and other countries with executive officers serving on FILA's Board as the problem. He cited the failure of their leaders to protect man's oldest sport. It was not the first, nor would it be the last time that Schalles called out wrestling's hierarchy.

Months later, Jim Scherr would take a broad view of the situation and note that, "...wrestling was in large part thrown off because of no political strength at the IOC, little respect for Martinetti, and Martinetti's lack of participation in the process, and arrogance towards the IOC process."

In the end, it really didn't matter who or what was to blame for wrestling's threatened expulsion from the Games. The Americans and Russians knew that certain things had to be fixed — pronto. New FILA leadership was paramount to any effort to retain wrestling's spot on the Olympic program. Women needed greater representation in the competition weight classes and in the FILA governance structure. Athletes deserved to be given more say in the sport. Rules and scoring had to be revised to support more action-packed matches. The sport needed better promotion and support from corporate sponsors. And... FILA and the national federations had to pay a lot more attention to the IOC.

CHAPTER 5 / **Phuket... The FILA Vote**

JUST THREE DAYS after the IOC Executive Board announced their verdict, the 22 FILA Bureau (Board) delegates gathered to meet at the Duangjitt Resort hotel in Phuket, Thailand for their regularly scheduled executive meeting. The Bureau serves as the directing and administrating body of FILA and is composed of the President, four Vice-Presidents, the General Secretary, 11 other elected members and the Presidents of the five Continental Councils.

During those three intervening days, it became apparent to the United States and Russian delegates, Stan Dziedzic and Mikhail Mamiashvili, that the only hope that wrestling had in changing the minds, and votes, of the IOC Executive Board members was to quickly replace Raphael Martinetti as the President of FILA. It would not be easy. Martinetti had his cronies on the Bureau.

Both Dziedzic and Mamiashvili had the strong support of their wrestling federations back home. For years, both the U.S. and Russian federation people were leery of Martinetti's ways and had heard whispers of a lack of harmony between Martinetti and his neighbors in Switzerland, the IOC.

Dziedzic talks about the general atmosphere going into the meeting. "I knew it was going to be contentious. While Martinetti had his followers, there were numerous people who had bad feelings towards him. Those feelings were percolating... escalating. The Rules Committee people, particularly, had problems with him. He put so many restrictive governors on us that we were handcuffed in making substantive changes."

Before the first day of the meeting Dziedzic, a freestyle World champion, and Mamiashvili, an Olympic Greco-Roman champion, met together briefly and agreed to try to convince Martinetti to resign.

Martinetti gave his opening address and it was evident that he wanted to stay

American Stan Dziedzic and Russian Mikhail Mamiashvili teamed up to convince a slim majority of FILA Bureau members to side against Martinetti in a hotly contested vote.

in control. Dziedzic told Martinetti in front of the group, "I never questioned your motives, Raphy, but the IOC has sent us a message. It has killed us. We are not even going to get an audience with them unless we make substantive changes."

Some of Martinetti's supporters were taken back by Dziedzic's frankness.

On one occasion Martinetti got up and threatened to leave when two Vice-Presidents — Tomiaki Fukoda and Matteo Pellicone — jumped up and prevented him from exiting the meeting. Dziedzic hinted that he was hoping they'd let him go. They convinced Martinetti to stay and for hours the group went back and forth as they discussed the leadership issue.

Mamiashvili strongly criticized Martinetti for having failed to follow recommendations that had been made to him by Bureau members. The President denied the accusations, saying that he had always worked in the best interests of FILA and always respected Bureau members by listening to their views.

Those who wanted to keep Martinetti blamed all the problems on the IOC. "Don't change generals in the middle of the battle," was a cry of support. Some delegates saw this confrontation as a personal attack and didn't want to see Martinetti hurt. There was some fear of the unknown as to who the next President might be. There were Bureau members on the fence. The group agreed to adjourn and reconvene the next day.

That evening Dziedzic spent several hours on the phone with USA Wrestling people back in the States discussing strategies for the following day. Mamiashvili tried to personally convince individual Bureau members that Martinetti had to go if wrestling were to have any chance of remaining in the Olympic program.

On the morning of the second day, Dziedzic tried out a new strategy, one that he had spent hours contemplating during that sleepless night. He offered to resign his own Vice-President position if Pellicone and Martinetti also quit. "I wanted to show the group that it was not personal on my part, nor was it a coup," explained Dziedzic. "Simply speaking, it was vital, in fact essential, to completely change the leadership of the organization."

Martinetti did not agree to Dziedzic's proposal. At that point Dziedzic indicated, "I was worried. He must have felt that he had the necessary support from the Bureau."

Martinetti insisted, "I need a vote of confidence."

Dziedzic was suspicious. "Deep down, Martinetti must have felt that he had 15 or so of the 21 votes in favor of keeping him in power." Dziedzic felt, "It should have been three, but it was probably more like 12."

Martinetti turned the meeting over to Pellicone of Italy to take the voice vote and left the room.

Meeting Room Table Seating Arrangement

	Italy	France	
Japan			USA
Korea			Turkey
Korea			Turkey
Guatemala			Morocco
Bulgaria			Qatar
Azerbaijan			Greece
Serbia			Uzbekistan
Russia			Russia
Hungary			Kazakhstan
			Oceania

At the head of the table General Secretary Michel Dusson of France and Italy's Pellicone are shoo-in votes for Martinetti. Japan's Fukoda leads off the open roll-call voting, which goes counter-clockwise around the table.

Fukuda casts his vote for Martinetti to remain as President of FILA.

So does Korea (twice) as does Continental President Francisco Lee Lopez from Guatemala. It is 6-0 for Martinetti after the first six votes.

Tzeno Tzenov of Bulgaria breaks the string with a vote against.

Azerbaijan votes for him... so it is 7-1.

Nenad Lalovic of Serbia and Russia's Mamiashvili, as expected, vote against —

there's still a chance to remove Martinetti.

However, when Hungary and Oceania vote for him the odds look real slim. It is 9-3. With nine votes to go, only two more YES votes are needed for Martinetti to stay in command.

Akhroldjan Ruzievof of Kazakhstan votes against. So does Natashia Yariguina of Russia.

Uzbekistan votes against. It is now 9-6 for Martinetti and there's still a chance, however slim.

Theodoros Hamakos of Greece votes against. Some say this was a shocker for Martinetti's supporters.

Qatar's Zamel Al Shahrani votes against. Another blow! As a newly elected Bureau member it was assumed Zamel would lean towards Martinetti, but to the chagrin of Martinetti, Zamel was much more astute.

Mohammed Ibnou Zahir of Morocco votes against.

Two votes from Turkey delegates are next up, with the tally at 9-9.

Rodica Yaksi gets it done, and votes against Martinetti.

That was the decisive one.

Some present at the meeting indicated that Dziedzic was sitting next to Turkey's Ayik and whispered to him just before his vote, "Ahmet, don't do it; for the sake of wrestling don't vote for him."

Ayik votes — FOR Martinetti... 10-10

Dziedzic is up. He smiles.

With an obvious sense of relief Dziedzic emphatically states, "No."

By one vote Martinetti fails to win the vote of confidence he most certainly expected.

Pellicone then starts to run the vote around the table once again — in the other direction. This time Dziedzic leads off with his "No" vote and everyone confirms their original vote. Dziedzic recalls, "Following the second vote we start arguing as a group. I interrupt. The vote stands — 11 against Martinetti continuing as FILA President, 10 for him. Martinetti has said that if he doesn't get the vote of confidence that he will resign. Someone needs to go out and tell Raphy that he did not get his vote of confidence. I'm sure he will then resign as he said he would."

Martinetti returns to the room. He hears that he lost the vote, 11-10. He talks about giving 50 years of his life to the sport with a touch of sentiment but says that he can't lead FILA without the confidence of the group. "I resign," he defiantly announces and storms out. As he's leaving he can't resist sharing some of his mind with Mamiashvili. Think, no love lost there.

Just one vote...

CHAPTER 6 / **Meet Nenad Lalovic**

AND JUST like that, FILA had to find a new, inspiring President to take on the daunting leadership responsibilities during the most turbulent of times in the 3,000-year history of wrestling. Sitting around the Bureau conference table in Phuket, where the echo of Raphy Martinetti's abrupt resignation was still resonating, no one leapt to sit in the President's chair. No one started campaigning for the job — though four or five candidates reportedly received initial consideration from their brethren.

Stan Dziedzic recalls, "In a very practical sense, as a group we looked around the room at all the FILA Bureau members to see who could fill the President position from a practical standpoint – like, who had the time to immediately take over these responsibilities on a full-time basis, move to FILA headquarters in Vevey and/or commute regularly from their home, and be able to travel across the world and back constantly during the next seven months. Then, among those who passed that test, identify who was the best qualified.

"In the end the group decided that either Nenad Lalovic or I were the two plausible choices. I indicated that, as an American and all of the attendant baggage that comes along with that, it would be disingenuous to pretend it would be in the best interest of wrestling for me to be the face of wrestling," said Dziedzic.

"That had to be Lalovic.

"I explained that my skill set was not a good fit – I only speak English, for example. However, I would not allow FILA to go without leadership, but only if Lalovic agreed to be the co-president and the face-of-FILA. Fortunately, Lalovic agreed to take on the job of President. He indicated that he was already semi-retired, willing to turn over his business and devote all of the time necessary to run FILA."

Thus, the FILA Bureau selected Nenad Lalovic of Serbia as its interim President. His first act was to promote Dziedzic to be his assistant. Before adjourning the meeting, Lalovic strengthened his team as he led the initiative to add three new co-opted FILA Bureau members: Pedro Gama Filho of Brazil, Alexander Karelin of Russia, and Jim Scherr of the United States.

Reaction around the wrestling world to Lalovic's ascension was one of curiosity. Who is this man? Even wrestling insiders did not know much, if anything, about the congenial Serbian other than that he had been serving as a member of FILA's Bureau since 2006.

First of all, Lalovic never competed as a wrestler. He hailed from Serbia, not one of the world powers in wrestling. Serbia has never won an Olympic medal in wrestling and it only qualified one wrestler to compete in the 2012 London Olympics. (Momir Petkovic, a Serbian, won an Olympic gold for Yugoslavia in 1976 and four World medals.)

But Lalovic brought to the table a compelling and diverse background. He was born in Belgrade, Yugoslavia in 1958 yet he spent his youth living and moving about in many different countries and cultures. His father, Milos Lalovic, was a diplomat, serving as the Yugoslavian ambassador to Lebanon, Jordan, Syria, Tunisia, Belgium and Switzerland at different times in his career. Coincidently, Lalovic's uncle at one point taught the IOC President, Jacques Rogge.

Lalovic completed his high school studies in Geneva before returning to Belgrade to study mechanical engineering in college. He displayed his entrepreneurial and leadership skills while there as he opened and operated a travel agency. In succeeding years he would own a tennis club (Lalovic's favorite sport at the time) and manage a shampoo factory.

Along the way, thanks to his son Mylos, Lalovic developed a keen interest in wrestling. In the strife-filled decade of the 1990s for Serbians, Mylos started wrestling at a local club where an old friend of Lalovic served as the coach. As Lalovic began attending practices and matches, he became more knowledgeable and interested in the sport. One day the coach asked Lalovic if he would like to become involved in rebuilding the country's wrestling infrastructure. Lalovic agreed and soon assumed key leadership roles.

In 2000 he was named President of the Serbian Wrestling Federation. Then in 2002 Lalovic helped organize the first Junior European Championships in Greco-Roman wrestling, followed by the Senior European Championships in Belgrade the following year. Serbians medaled in both events for the first time in the history of their country. Lalovic has also served on the Bureaus of CELA, the European Wrestling Federation and the Serbian Olympic Committee.

Being proficient in five languages — Serbian, Russian, French, German and English — has clearly helped Lalovic navigate easily across borders with political and sports leaders. He is massive, but much more the teddy bear type rather than the muscular Eastern European nightclub bouncer type.

Lalovic (who has a penchant for smoking cigarettes as often as possible — proof that he's not a wrestler!) likely inherited his sense of diplomacy from his father. He has those innate leadership qualities that are essential if wrestling is to remain an Olympic sport. He listens carefully; he surrounds himself with the most capable people; he delegates; he's jovial and encouraging in an unassuming way; and he is not afraid of taking on an enormous challenge. He understands that time is of the essence.

When taking on the job as FILA President, Lalovic knew what he was getting into. Wrestling had to claw its way back into contention to remain an Olympic sport in 2020 and beyond. It had serious competition — the other seven sports jostling for the one open spot had each been working on their bid for at least two years. Lalovic and his team had just three months to turn things around and prepare a winning presentation for the IOC Executive Board in Russia in May. Lalovic had the support of his Bureau, though Martinetti and his group of cronies were still lurking as Bureau members representing the old way. He needed right from the start to change the culture within FILA — the immediate need for transparency and open communication within the Bureau and with the score of wrestling federations and followers around the world.

Lalovic understood that despite wrestling's strong heritage it had to right itself in the eyes of the IOC. It had to embrace change — right away. Among the most urgent changes Lalovic foresaw were the creation or reform of a number of federation commissions, including bringing in active athletes into the athletes commission, more involvement of women on the management side and the competition side, as well as dramatic rule changes. He vowed to make wrestling more understandable and attractive for its spectators and competitors. In addition, Lalovic pledged to upgrade the sport's relations with the media and to devote attention to the promotion and marketing of the sport worldwide.

He also wisely took the humble path. In a Reuters interview Lalovic revealed what he told IOC President Rogge when they met in March: "I pointed out the fact that we were going in a wrong direction in the last few years and that we in no way blame the decision of the IOC for our predicament and will view its decision as an opportunity to improve our sport and to help strengthen the Olympic movement. We have to fix the problems we have in wrestling."

Lalovic was undertaking the most difficult job of his life, although on the sur-

One of Lalovic's first orders of business was to schedule a meeting with IOC President Rogge and to assume the blame for wrestling's predicament.

face his mission looked simple. "I have to keep wrestling in the Olympics," he said on more than one occasion. He was also wise enough to know how his report card as a FILA Bureau leader would be graded — if the IOC voted to keep wrestling as an Olympic sport, he'd be awarded an A.

Anything less, it's an F.

CHAPTER 7 / **Tehran... A Perfect Storm**

AS THE Team Leader for the USA women's freestyle team, Noel Thompson was in Cuba on February 12, supporting the United States wrestlers competing in the Granma-Cerro Pelado International Wrestling tournament, when he heard the startling news. USA men's freestyle coach Zeke Jones told Thompson that the IOC had just recommended that wrestling be cut from the Olympic Games.

"Like everyone else, I couldn't believe it," said Thompson, who is CEO of the Thompson Global hedge fund. "I thought it was an early April Fools joke. After a few seconds to catch my breath, I understood... it was true. I felt just terrible. It was like someone punched me in the stomach."

Thompson made a quick decision. He originally intended to fly directly from Cuba to Iran to attend the men's World Cup matches the following week. He changed his plans and immediately returned home to New York City so that he could better understand the reasons behind, and the consequences of, the IOC's recommendation.

Back in New York, Thompson spent a day talking with several close confidants about wrestling's grave situation. He also treated his wife to a special dinner. It was, after all, February 14, Valentine's Day.

The following day Thompson headed off to Tehran, Iran. Just a week after the IOC Executive Board's stunning recommendation, the world's top men's freestyle teams were gathering there to compete in the FILA World Cup, an annual 10-team international event with a dual-meet format.

While jetting oversees he reflected back to four years earlier when the freestyle World Cup was last held in Iran. The USA was not even invited to that event since they did not place high enough in the previous year's (2008) Olympic Games. The whole premise was different in February, 2013. Fortunately, the USA men's freestyle team captured two gold and one bronze medal at the 2012 Olympics; thus, this year they were more than welcome to participate with nine other nations in this premier tournament.

"Having the United States competing in the tournament along with the world's most powerful wrestling nations — Russia and Iran — was the first wave of a perfect storm that would eventually unfold," commented Thompson. "I could see where Tehran would become the starting point from where the international wrestling community comes together to fight back against the IOC recommendation."

Competition included four days of Greco-Roman and freestyle wrestling — February 19-22. Coincidentally, during this period world powers were conducting significant negotiations regarding Tehran's nuclear program. Journalists and correspondents from the major media outlets such as CNN and ABC were reporting on-site from Tehran at the time. Some would turn their attention to the story-line coming from the wrestling arena.

Remarkably, televisions and newspapers were showing wrestlers and coaches from the United States, Russia and Iran locked arm-in-arm in the arena protesting the damning IOC recommendation, while politicians and diplomats from those three nations could not find their way to a nuclear arms agreement.

"The stars were aligning," says Thompson, who wrestled for Hofstra a decade ago.

Before, between and after the wrestling matches, there were frequent meetings between the major wrestling federation administrators from the United States, Russia, Iran, Turkey, Azerbaijan, Japan and so on. All the significant FILA players were on hand. "Tehran was the first opportunity after the Phuket FILA meetings for the wrestling leaders to come together and decide how they best marshal themselves going forward to save Olympic wrestling," said Thompson. "From wrestling's standpoint, the timing could not have been better."

At the matches, sellout crowds of 15,000 boisterous fans jammed the arena so full that a fire marshal in the U.S. would not have been pleased. The aisles were packed with enthusiastic fans who were virtually stacked on top of each other.

The massive crowd rose to its feet and cameras flashed across the arena when athletes from each team were called to the center of the mat during the opening ceremonies.

The roars from the crowd were so loud it was drowning out the public address announcer. As the athletes lined the mat, one representative from each team was called to the center. Athletes from each country came together to hold a banner

America's Jordan Burroughs scores another takedown in the World Cup matches.
Hamid Forootan

that read...

THE OLYMPICS WITHOUT WRESTLING… NEVER, NEVER!

During the event, fans also held signs in both Farsi (the national language of Iran) and in English reading: "Keep Olympic Wrestling" and "We Are All Wrestling People."

During a three-plus hour break before the medal round, with no athletes or coaches in the arena, Iranian fans remained in the stands. The fans continued to cheer, chant, wave huge Iranian flags, beat drums and play horns. Their trademark chant of *do-ta-da-loo-ta-do-Iran!* continued to be heard as fans also enthusiastically stomped their feet.

The event featured high-level wrestling, but also included great shows of respect and sportsmanship between competing countries. Wrestlers from Iran shook hands and hugged American wrestlers following each match in their dual, which was won by the home team.

"We have absolutely zero problems with the countries being unified on saving wrestling," U.S. National team coach Zeke Jones said. "When we arrived in Tehran for the World Cup, the Iranians had their arms wide open to our wrestling program and to Americans because they realize that it's a better world with us together.

TEHRAN... A PERFECT STORM 41

The then President of Iran, Mahmoud Ahmadinejad, presents the USA wrestling team with their third place medal at the World Cup in Tehran.

"The countries here will do anything in working together to keep Olympic wrestling in the program. We have the same goal and the same belief and passion about the sport of wrestling," said Jones.

Two-time U.S. World team member Brent Metcalf sensed a much different feeling between athletes and teams in Iran than he had experienced at previous international events. "You could see there was a lot more friendship between countries," he said. "There is a lot more communication now between countries because we can all sympathize with each other. We all lost something that is very dear to wrestling, which is the opportunity to wrestle in the Olympic Games."

Despite the outward signs of friendship, the World Cup wrestlers competing for the United States were feeling just a little more than the usual competitive pressure. Thompson explains, "It was imperative to the overall cause that the United States earns a medal at this multi-team tournament. The USA had to be right up there on the medal stand with Russia and Iran. Anything less and it just wouldn't be the same sign of solidarity.

"Our guys had to perform to help save the sport. We'd be receiving no handshakes from the President of Iran if we didn't make it to the stand," said Thompson.

The American freestylers came through, in a big way. During the first day of

Rich Bender and his counterpart at the Iranian Wrestling Federation, Hojatollah Khatib, were all hugs after they worked out details for the Iranian team's visit to New York City in May.

wrestling, the USA team defeated Georgia and Japan, but lost to ever-tough Iran, 6-1. Only Jordan Burroughs came away with a victory for the USA against the Iranians.

On the second day the U.S. fought back, shutting out Bulgaria to reach the bronze medal match against Belarus. While Iran and Russia competed for the gold, which Iran won, six Americans — Obe Blanc, Jimmy Kennedy, Brent Metcalf, Burroughs, Max Askren and Tervel Diagnev — each beat their Belarus opponent to earn the coveted bronze medal for the United States.

Iran, Russia and the USA teams took to the podium. Flashbulbs and video cameras were on full throttle as the President of Iran, Mahmoud Ahmadinejad, shook the hand of each American wrestler and coach. Perhaps an IOC Executive Board member caught one of those telling photos or videos, along with millions of people around the world.

Thompson's vision of the three world wrestling powers standing together on the podium, shaking hands and hugging each other while being enthusiastically cheered by the host Iranian crowd, had come to fruition.

Burroughs, who could walk down most U.S. streets and go relatively unnoticed, became a virtual rock star during the World Cup. Even though Burroughs defeated Iran's Sadegh Goudarzi in the 2011 World finals and 2012 Olympic finals, he was still showered with favorable cheers and chants when he competed.

After his last match, Burroughs had to navigate his way through a sea of fans outside on his way to the team bus. U.S. assistant coach Bill Zadick grabbed Burroughs around the waist and helped him push his way through the crowd. Grown Iranian men, with flowing black beards, were trying to draw close enough to get a photograph or an autograph of Burroughs.

"Wrestling in Iran was sweet — it was just a tremendous experience," Burroughs said. "Iran has the best wrestling fans in the world, bar none. I received more attention there than I receive on my home soil. It was kind of like being Justin Bieber with all the attention that I was getting. It was nuts."

President Ahmadinejad also was front and center during the event. Despite political differences and hostilities that exist between Iran and America, Ahmadinejad presented Jones with his team's trophy after the U.S. finished in third place. The Iranian President also smiled, shook hands and posed for photos with the American team after the event.

"No matter your political feelings, that was a testament to the influence of our great sport," Zadick said. "The World Cup was an awesome display. It showed how our sport brings people of all sizes, races, religions and walks of life together. It builds bridges between people and governments that might be politically opposed. Where else do you see a controversial world leader presenting a trophy to a sports team from the USA? It also showed how competitors and fans develop mutual respect for one another and band together with a common goal for a right cause."

Rich Bender had made two previous trips to Iran for major wrestling events, but he said this trip was unique. "The World Cup was so critical because it set the tone for this whole Olympic fight," Bender said. "It immediately brought the issue to a wider audience than we normally could have if we had not had the World Cup right after the initial IOC vote. We had an expanded opportunity to impact and communicate to the world that wrestling provides unique opportunities for difference cultures to come together for the common good of wrestling.

"What was demonstrated at the World Cup was that the sport of wrestling was not going to sit back and let this happen. The countries are all very determined to keep this sport in the Olympics and we are all going to stand up and fight for this. There was a tremendous show of unity, camaraderie and brotherhood between the 10 countries that took part in the World Cup. I had never seen anything like it.

"This event was up a notch from what I had experienced before in Iran. That was as electric an environment as I've ever seen for wrestling," said Bender.

Leading up to the World Cup, Bender and Amir Bashiri, USA Wrestling's liaison with Iran, were in discussions with Hojatollah Khatib, President of the Iran Wrestling Federation, to bring the Iranians to America to support the Keep Olympic Wrestling effort. Bender explains, "I spoke with Mike Novogratz to get the agreement to invite [the Iran wrestling team] to the New York Beat-the-Streets Gala before I went to Tehran. It was during the World Cup when I publicly invited the Iranians to bring their team to New York."

Even though it was less than two months away, the Iranians accepted the offer and promised that they would come to America, along with the Russian team, to demonstrate solidarity amongst these three ideologically opposite nations and send a compelling message to the IOC... that wrestling should remain in the Games.

"Those days in Tehran were an once-in-a-lifetime experience for me," says Thompson. "I was part of a team telling the world our story about wrestling. I saw myself elevated as an ambassador for the sport. What happened in Tehran really ignited the wrestling movement going forward. It gave the sport the legs it needed to organize and execute its plan to win back the IOC vote. The marketing campaign began then."

CHAPTER 8 / **Building the Team**

FROM Afghanistan to Zimbabwe, 177 countries maintain a national wrestling federation (such as USA Wrestling) operating under the FILA umbrella. There is no doubt that the news of the IOC Executive Board's outrageous recommendation was a cause for anguish and concern in each of these nations. From those 177 countries, one grabbed the leadership role in developing and executing the game plan to do whatever it took to change the minds of the all-powerful IOC voters — the United States of America.

This is not to say that other countries didn't mount their own form of protest while trying to achieve restitution. Within hours of the IOC announcement, cries for signing and sending petitions to the IOC came from several corners. Japan and the USA instigated online signups, each with a goal of obtaining 100,000 names. After 90 days, the USA had garnered 72,000 signatures — Japan claimed 950,000 of them.

Russia developed as a strong team player in the days to come. The chairman of the Russian Olympic Committee, Alexander Zhukov, said that he intended to appeal to the IOC to reverse their recommendation to remove wrestling from the list of core Olympic sports. Vladimir Putin, the Russian President, announced that he would fight on every level to secure wrestling's Olympic future, a stance backed by his Iranian counterpart, Mahmoud Ahmadinejad.

The President of Bulgaria, Rossen Plevneliev, also spoke out in favor of keeping wrestling in the Olympic Games. In a letter sent to the Bulgarian Wrestling Federation, Plevneliev wrote, "I categorically support all efforts towards keeping wrestling an Olympic sport."

In addition, the Association of Summer Olympic International Federations as

USA Wrestling leaders Rich Bender (left) and Jim Ravannack (right) were delighted when Mike Novogratz immediately volunteered to raise money to support the fight.

well as the Association of National Olympic Committees threw their support behind wrestling's efforts to remain a core Olympic sport.

Meanwhile, the U.S. Olympic Committee CEO Scott Blackmun would only go so far as to say that wrestling should be a part of the Olympics — but not at the expense of softball (a sport competing with wrestling for the one open Olympic slot in 2020 and 2024).

And while the U.S. Senate passed bi-partisan legislation urging the IOC to reverse its recommendation, there was nary a word on the subject coming from the White House. Some wrestling people were privately talking about "a lack of courage" on the part of the USOC and the most senior diplomats in the U.S.

But the people at the top of United States wrestling circles were immediately on the attack. John Bardis, a Board member of USA Wrestling from 1997 to 2011, described his initial reactions in an interview with *USA Wrestler*: "The American wrestling community reacted very quickly. My reaction after being very angry was we have to get Jim Scherr involved. He needed to provide insight into the IOC. Jim is the most vastly experienced senior Olympics sports executive who has been a Senior

wrestler in history.

"I called Jim immediately and said I don't know where this is headed but you need to lead this effort. You need to be at the front of the class on this. Jim understands the tributaries and the nuances of the Olympic movement at the IOC level. So does his twin brother, Bill, particularly with his experience as an Olympian but also being the lead guy on the ground with the 2016 bid in Chicago. Instantly, it was pretty clear we needed to have that kind of insight and expertise leading the team."

With their combined athletic and business backgrounds, Bardis and the Scherr brothers brought enormous strength to the cause. Bardis' connection to Olympic wrestling stretches over four decades, starting with his third-place finish at the 1976 Greco-Roman Olympic Trials. He was the Team Leader for the USA 2005-07 Greco World teams and the 2008 Olympic team. Bardis is the founder and CEO of MedAssets, a highly-successful Georgia-based professional services provider to the healthcare industry. He was named among the 100 most influential people in healthcare in the U.S. in 2013 by *Modern Healthcare* magazine.

The Scherr brothers are natives of South Dakota who wrestled collegiately at the University of Nebraska. Bill's resume includes such highlights as: NCAA champion at Nebraska in 1984; U.S National Senior champion in both freestyle (five times) and Greco-Roman; FILA World freestyle champion in 1985; Olympic bronze medalist in 1988; Vice-President at Goldman-Sachs; leader of the Chicago 2016 Olympic bid team. In February, 2012 he joined Barclays Wealth as a Director, specializing in equity portfolio management.

Bill's twin brother Jim's list of accomplishments and responsibilities in the sports world is unparalleled: NCAA wrestling champion for Nebraska in 1984; Olympian and World silver and bronze medalist; Executive Director of USA Wrestling from 1990-2000; various leadership roles at the United States Olympic Committee, including CEO from 2005-09; founder and CEO of the 776 Original Marketing firm in Colorado Springs; and, since January, 2012 the first commissioner of the National Collegiate Hockey Conference. Scherr is now COO of the 2015 European Games in Baku, Azerbaijan.

During the first 12 hours after the IOC announcement Bardis, the Scherr brothers and Bender started putting together their plan. Based on conversations they had with several IOC Executive Board members and the IOC Director General, Christophe DeKepper, they laid out their initial public relations strategy and the essential need to get rid of Martinetti. The PR strategy early on was not to give in to the temptation to attack the IOC, but to position the decision as an opportunity for wrestling.

The group understood that they needed to raise money to fund the ideas they had in mind. Bardis agreed to take charge of the finances and reached out to Mike

BUILDING THE TEAM 49

Despite their full-time jobs as senior business executives, John Bardis and Bill Scherr found time to work intensely for wrestling's salvation from the start.

Novogratz, an ex-Princeton University wrestler. 'Novo' is considered a Wall Street tycoon — a former Goldman Sachs salesman and trader who is a principal with the Fortress Investment Group — and is President of Beat-the-Streets in New York City.

Novogratz was in Switzerland at the time of the IOC announcement, which he heard about from a taxi driver. He came right aboard and within 24 hours of the damning recommendation, Novogratz and his growing group of allies raised $500,000. In the following two weeks, the total contributions exceeded $1 million.

By the end of February, Ravannack and Bender had formalized their volunteer working group, called the Coalition for the Preservation of Olympic Wrestling (CPOW), an impressive team of U.S. business and wrestling leaders whose mission was to ensure that wrestling remains as a core sport of the Olympic Games.

The original makeup of the Committee included: Chairperson Bill Scherr; Spokesperson Mike Novogratz; Director of Development/Finance John Bardis. Other committee members included: Andy Barth, Rich Bender, Clarissa Chun, Mike DerGarabedian, Roger Frizzell, Dan Gable, Rulon Gardner, Jeff Levitetz, Art Martori, Kerry McCoy, James Ravannack, Jim Scherr, John Smith and Lee Roy Smith. Wes Battle was recruited and named CPOW Chief of Staff in early April. Meanwhile, USA Wrestling added Mike Rosati to its national staff in the position of USA Wrestling/CPOW Executive Liaison. In late June, Rosati was promoted to CPOW Chief of Operations. CPOW hired Jim Scherr as a professional consultant. All others on the Committee served as volunteers.

Fundraising for CPOW was a challenge at first because the donors did not know exactly where their contributions were going. They knew, however, that their sport was on the brink and they showed their passion for and confidence in the cause through their wallets. The list of most generous donors included Jim Ravannack, Mike Novogratz, John Bardis, Andy Barth, Jamie Dinan, Jeff Levitetz, John Paul Tudor, Ed Gallegos, All-American Wrestling Supply & Cliff Keen Athletic, National Wrestling Hall of Fame, Billy Baldwin, Steve Friedman, Andy Lago, Alan Meltzer, Bill & Jim Scherr, Rich Tavoso, David Pottruck, Cliff Fretwell, Al Bevilacqua, and Rich Battle.

When asked why he would take on the assignment of CPOW leader in addition to his full-time position at Barclay's, Bill Scherr responded, "I want to see wrestling remain a part of the Olympic Games. The Olympics are meaningful to the sport of wrestling and wrestling can make a meaningful contribution to the Olympics. I love wrestling, I love the Olympics, and I want to see the two stay associated with each other, which is why I accepted the role of working with CPOW."

Under Scherr's crack leadership, the CPOW team ran like a Swiss watch. One-to-three-hour Saturday morning conference calls kept all members updated and provided the means for discussing strategy and tactics as a well-informed, intensely motivated volunteer group. Everyone was on board, sharing the same mission and goals.

Ravannack elected to play a supportive rather than a lead role in the CPOW program. "I helped pick the leaders of the effort and then let them do what they needed to do," said the successful businessman from Louisiana. He played an important role, though, in working with the 51 state leaders of USA Wrestling's State Chapters. Ravannack met with every State Chairman and implored each chapter to contribute to the cause, according to their means. Every single state made a donation — many of them significant. Georgia led the way with a $25,000 donation. Other states that made the most generous financial contributions were Idaho, Indiana, Texas, Minnesota, Illinois, New Jersey, Kansas, Louisiana, Nebraska, Utah and Ohio.

Gable took on an active role as a member of CPOW and described his effort as "all-consuming". He was seen virtually everywhere, supporting and promoting the drive to keep wrestling on the Olympic program.

"Wrestling belongs in the Olympic Games," he said. "People associate the Olympics with sports like running and swimming and wrestling. If you take wrestling out of the Olympics, it would be a huge setback for that event. Wrestling means a lot to people all over the world. It's an ancient art that has been part of the Olympics forever.

"On the international level, wrestling had a heart attack but did not die," Gable said. "We finally hit a thread or an artery or vein that goes to the heart that got cut off. The bottom line is that we have to improve circulation."

As the fight to save wrestling intensified in the spring, additional members joined the CPOW team, which became a part of USA Wrestling. It was not unusual to have 20-25 individuals on the Saturday morning conference call. Actor Billy Baldwin, a former high school and college wrestler, was one of those subsequently elected a member. Baldwin emerged as one of the heroes in the fight to keep wrestling in the Olympics. He provided valuable input and ideas on the weekly calls, and took a very active role with the USA-based group. "The Olympic Games without wrestling," Baldwin said, "is like the Fourth of July without fireworks.

"Wrestling instills the values of work ethic, discipline and mental toughness," he said. "The sport is important in turning young boys into men and young girls into women. If we lose wrestling in the Olympics it will be tragic for America as well as the entire world. There are eight-, nine- and 10-year-olds growing up in places like Russia, Iran, Azerbaijan, Greece, Turkey and Uzbekistan who already have Olympic dreams in their hearts and minds. It would be completely wrong and completely unjust to take that opportunity away from them."

Baldwin also organized an auction to raise money for the Olympic fight.

The monies that CPOW was raising and the infrastructure that it was establishing had one primary objective in mind: provide the very best support to FILA in their preparation and delivery of wrestling's presentations to the IOC — first and foremost the one to the IOC Executive Board in May. Then, if successful in May, to the IOC general assembly in September.

This support would come in all shapes and sizes. A CPOW team established a website, a Facebook page and other social media outlets in order to communicate its plans to the millions of people in the worldwide wrestling community.

And CPOW, in conjunction with FILA, sought the expertise of several professional service firms in certain important areas where such outside assistance was deemed essential. These firms would play a key role in advising wrestling leadership in dealing with significant issues that seemed to arise on a daily basis, as well as with the public, the media and the IOC in the coming months.

The list included:

- KOM Sports Marketing, a Colorado Springs marketing firm headed by Steve Brunner.
- Ketchum, one of the largest public relations agencies in the world and New

York-based Weber Shandwick, the global public relations company that handled successful Olympic host bids for Beijing in 2008 and Sochi in 2014.
• The Frizzell Group, a public relations organization founded by Roger Frizzell, a 30-year industry leader and former All-American wrestler at the University of Oklahoma. Frizzell donated all of his valuable time to CPOW.
• Teneo Strategy, a premier global strategy consulting organization which specializes in the Olympic movement.
• TSE Consulting, a strategy consulting firm hired primarily to assist on FILA governance issues and in helping to develop a strategic plan for wrestling.
• The Craig Company LLC, professional lobbyist Andrew Craig's management consulting firm in Michigan. Craig was retained by the Russian Wrestling Federation.

CPOW and the Russian Wrestling Federation made the financial investment, along with FILA, to secure the services of these professional firms up through the final IOC general assembly vote in September. Reportedly, the original terms for covering Teneo's fees and expenses were 25% from CPOW, 25% from Russia and 50% from FILA. The original plan called for Jim Scherr to work as part of Teneo Strategy. Instead, Dziedzic negotiated a arrangement whereby CPOW would contribute less to Teneo's fees but cover all of Scherr's salary and some of his expenses as he worked in a more independent consulting relationship with the team.

In mid-March, Dziedzic, Jim Scherr, Andrew Craig and Terrence Burns of Teneo Strategy met for several days at John Bardis' office in Atlanta, Georgia. These sessions proved critical in developing and setting the sport's overarching strategy for the campaign during the next six months to keep wrestling in the Olympic Games. Jim Scherr states, "The strategy set in Atlanta is the core basis for the constitutional changes that FILA eventually implements."

Dziedzic, whose financial business background includes 10 years as the Managing Director of Lehman Brothers' Atlanta office, recalls, "These meetings helped lay the groundwork for our presentations in St. Petersburg and Buenos Aires and our lobbying agenda. We were working at the strategic level yet delving into things like the type of presentations and presenters for the IOC meetings; Lalovic's schedule; where and when to hold the Extraordinary Congress session; content to rewrite the IOC questionnaire; timeline to implement rules changes; governance issues. We agreed that TSE Consulting was the best choice to assist FILA in the governance area.

"John's assistant was at our service and John joined us the second day," Dziedzic said. "He provided valuable input into the process; his role on USADA's board proved helpful in a number of instances, including calls to contacts within the IOC. His ability to counteract forces to bring CPOW back on track was also helpful."

CPOW's charge was to oversee the effort within the United States as part of the massive international coalition being formed to retain wrestling in the Olympics. There was a delicate balance to play out. The United States needed to be the driver in this worldwide effort, yet also wanted to work closely with the international wrestling community, especially FILA and the Russian Wrestling Federation.

Wrestling leaders in Russia made significant investments in the movement. Ravannack points out that besides helping to fund the consultants, they also provided superior services, manpower and support totaling millions of dollars during the two critical gatherings in May on their home turf — the Extraordinary FILA Congress meeting in Moscow and the IOC Executive vote in St. Petersburg. This was in no small part due to the solid relationships built over time between Dziedzic and Mamiashvili at the FILA Bureau, and Bender and his Russian counterparts at the national federation level.

CPOW set up a structure of committees and subcommittees, the groups who would be working on specific areas of the overall effort. Three committees were established to handle: 1) International Relations, led by Jim Scherr and Bender; 2) Public Relations and Marketing, led by Frizzell and Gary Abbott; 3) Development and Finance, led by Bardis and Larry Nugent.

CPOW Committee members talked with each other daily; assumed specific responsibilities; worked closely with the consultants; made and reviewed plans going forward; interfaced with FILA representatives, particularly Dziedzic, the USA delegate.

Meanwhile, active groups were working behind the scenes on formulating the American recommendations for changes to the international wrestling rules. Working with Bill Scherr and Dan Gable, the USA Wrestling National coaches Zeke Jones, Steve Fraser and Terry Steiner formed subcommittees within their style to address this issue. Acting FILA president Lalovic indicated that this would be a most important focus of the FILA Congress meeting in Moscow in May.

The objectives of this committee included recommending rule changes that promoted: 1) simple for spectators to understand; 2) increases action; 3) rewards risk-taking; 4) allows no bias into officiating; 5) allows the best athlete to win; 6) is exciting for television viewing.

This would turn out to be a rather complex and controversial issue — domestically and internationally.

CHAPTER 9 / **Meet the Press**

ONE OF the most important contributions that CPOW/USA Wrestling made to the international effort was the introduction of Bob Condron as an interim FILA Press Officer. Condron had recently retired, having worked more than 30 years as a public relations executive for the U.S. Olympic Committee. He also served for many years on the IOC Press Commission.

Condron was well liked and respected by many of the right people — at USA Wrestling and at the IOC. From his home in Colorado Springs, Condron phoned the USA Wrestling offices on February 12 when he heard the disturbing news about Olympic wrestling and offered his assistance. "I told them I'd be happy to help if they need me," recalls Condron. A few days later he started working with Gary Abbott and Craig Sesker in the Communications Department of USA Wrestling.

"It was a crazy situation," said Condron. "For two weeks or so I was working with Gary on communications stuff. One morning, Rich Bender calls me in his office and says, 'I just talked with the FILA people and suggested to them that they bring you on board. Can you go live and work in Switzerland as the FILA Press Officer?'"

"When?" I asked.

"Two days from now," Bender replied.

"I told Bender that I had to talk with my wife and that I'd get back to him shortly. She said 'okay' and sure enough two days later I was flying to Geneva, Switzerland where I met up with Stan Dziedzic to start this odyssey of a new career."

FILA had never had a Press Officer. Many believe that its abysmal lack of communications directly led to the IOC disaster. FILA's Dziedzic admits: "Our

Bob Condron discusses media strategy with wrestling correspondent T.R. Foley and CPOW Chief of Staff Wes Battle in Buenos Aires during the IOC General Assembly session in September.

communications, both internal and external, were lousy. Even inside the sport we had no information. We were just told everything was okay — but clearly it was not."

Condron started working out of his assigned room, adjacent to Rue du Chateau 6, better known as 'the 'castle', which FILA owned as its office building. After the first few days on the job, he commandeered castle office space where the Japanese bid committee had set up shop for when they needed space. It wasn't ideal from a functional standpoint, but at least it was workable.

Condron brought a whole new attitude and media relations approach to FILA. In the past, most everything was secretive; meetings were held behind closed doors; no media people were kept informed; Board members were left in the dark, as were national federation leaders. In fact, Condron found that there was little public relations infrastructure in place at FILA headquarters. "There were no mailing lists, no photographs, no archives, no clippings, nothing when it comes to the press. I basically had to start from scratch."

He also brought with him some important contacts. One of Condron's past associates from the IOC met Dziedzic and him in Lausanne upon their arrival from Geneva on March 4. Together they arranged introductory meetings for Condron, Dziedzic and Lalovic over the next several days with key IOC leaders. On the evening of Condron's arrival, Lalovic also arrived at FILA headquarters and met Condron for the first time at dinner. For the next week Condron started to demonstrate his worth as the acting President was inundated with distractions — Lalovic was grateful for Condron's assistance.

It was at these early March meetings when FILA began to understand some of the specific tactics that the IOC was requiring from wrestling. Dziedzic recalls, "It was clear from the very first meeting on March 5th with the IOC that keeping all three wrestling disciplines (Greco-Roman, men's freestyle and women's freestyle) with seven weight classes each — though that was FILA's quest — was not going to be realistic. That would have increased the number of weight classes competing to 21, rather than keeping it at 18, as in the last three Olympics. If wrestling hoped to be a member in good standing in the Olympic Games beyond 2016, we had to figure out a way to increase women's participation without increasing the total amount of competitors. The IOC wasn't going to tell us how to solve that riddle."

Just a week after Condron's arrival at FILA, Lalovic attended a private meeting that he had previously scheduled with IOC President Rogge. Working with IOC spokesman Mike Adams, whom Condron knew from his days at the USOC, Condron arranged all the press coordination for this heralded event. It received worldwide coverage. He was gaining Lalovic's trust and confidence.

Condron remembers his conversation with Lalovic: "I told him that it was important for the media to know about his meeting with the IOC President. That's how the rest of the world will learn that wrestling is taking the offensive in its quest to retain an Olympic berth. Lalovic allowed me to set up a press conference for him at FILA headquarters after the meeting and we received some decent coverage. That never would have happened under Martinetti — or even his predecessors. It was ingrained at FILA headquarters that the media was foreign.

"I wanted people to see the changes being made at FILA — and the media was integral to making that happen," said Condron. "I believed that FILA had to continually drive home the message that it was making the necessary changes in order to remain an Olympic sport."

Within days, Condron was helping formulate FILA's media strategy moving forward. Lalovic's schedule was becoming more demanding by the week and Condron was there to assist him in fashioning his message and arranging press meetings everywhere he went.

The importance of these early meetings with IOC personnel, from Rogge on down, cannot be overstated. For once, FILA was listening and learning rather than the Martinetti-esque style of going about business despite what the rulers of the Games (yes, the IOC) deemed necessary. FILA was learning about the seriousness on the IOC's part about gender equity; the voice of the athlete; a governance issue regarding their officials' organization; and modernization issues regarding television ratings — all items where the IOC was suggesting changes.

It soon became apparent that the FILA strategy to remain as an Olympic sport hinged upon three pillars...

• Listen to what the IOC had to say;
• Make sweeping changes to many aspects of wrestling which were long overdue;
• Communicate, communicate, communicate — through the media and the social networks with the world, and through personal relationships with IOC staff and members.

The appointment of Condron would prove to be a watershed event in wrestling's comeback efforts.

CHAPTER 10 / Spreading the Good News

I N THE spring of 2013 the five Continental Groups within FILA held their Presidential elections. Since the Presidents of each one of the Continental Groups sit on FILA's Bureau, there was always more than passing interest in the outcome of these elections. And even more so in this tumultuous year for wrestling where a FILA Bureau voter could exert extraordinary power in casting a vote FOR or AGAINST the many changes being put forward.

To complicate matters, at the same time — not so coincidentally — Raphy Martinetti's head was resurfacing. When Martinetti resigned as FILA President in February, most of the wrestling community believed he was history and gave a collective sigh of relief. But the deposed chief had other ideas. He was not going away. The former FILA President was threatening to make an appeal to the Court of Arbitration for Sport (CAS) to regain his position as head of FILA. Naturally, this was a major distraction and threat for Nenad Lalovic. Martinetti was also arranging to attend the Continental Group election meetings to seek support for his campaign to re-establish himself as President. Lalovic saw what Martinetti was up to; hence, he and his supporters deemed it necessary for him to attend these events as well.

Rumors were swirling around these meetings and elections. It was widely known that Martinetti only lost his vote of confidence in Phuket by a single vote. If one of the Continental Presidents who voted against Martinetti in Phuket lost his Continental election and was replaced on the Bureau, well, that could tip the balance of power back to Martinetti. This made the Panama CPLA Continental meeting taking place between April 2-8 ever so important for Lalovic — and the future of Olympic wrestling.

Lalovic was hoping his visit would gain the support of Francisco Lee Lopez, the incumbent CPLA president from Guatamala who had earlier voted for Martinetti. Lalovic's presence at the Panama meetings proved to be a wise decision. While Lopez won re-election, Lalovic had a hand in swaying him closer to his camp. This would be an important factor later on as it looked as though sides were again being formed within the Bureau.

The Panama venue also served as the ideal time for new FILA Bureau member Jim Scherr to meet Lalovic, discuss strategic issues relating to the IOC and gain Lalovic's confidence. Having recently served as U.S. Olympic Committee Chief Executive Officer, Scherr was more familiar than anyone on FILA Bureau with the ways of the IOC.

In three weeks Scherr and Dziedzic would be representing FILA at the IOC's Sport for All international conference in Lima, Peru, where there would be more than a few IOC delegates in attendance. This would be the kickoff of wrestling meet-and-greet time. Lalovic wanted to make sure that FILA was properly spreading the message to the IOC delegates that wrestling was committed to making the changes necessary to regain its eligibility on the Olympic program. Scherr passed the Lalovic litmus test with flying colors.

Jim Scherr played a significant role in many aspects of the entire process even though he moved with his family to Baku midway through the effort.

Meanwhile, Bob Condron had Lalovic on the move and was letting the international press know of his whereabouts on a regular basis. For the last half of April alone, Condron scheduled Lalovic to give key speeches in far-away but strategically important gatherings, such as...

- AIPS Congress, Sochi, Russia, April 16-17
- Asian Championships, New Delhi, India, April 17-19
- African Championships, N'Djamena, Chad, April 29-May 2

The Asian and African Championships coincided with their Continental President elections. At the African Championships and election in Chad, the Moroccan, Zahir, who voted against Martinetti in Phuket, lost the Continental election and his place on the Board. Chalk one up for the Martinetti camp.

From a media standpoint, no gathering was more important than the AIPS (Association Internationale De La Presse Sportive or the International Sports Press Association) annual conference in Sochi. Addressing a crowd of leading sports journalists from around the globe, Lalovic talked about recognizing the necessity to make changes to improve the sport for the contestants and the fans — plus its need to modernize and market itself better.

Russia's President Vladimar Putin joined Lalovic in front of the press corps and proclaimed Russia's full support of keeping wrestling as an Olympic sport. Russian sports minister Vitaly Mutko and President of the Russian Wrestling Federation Mikhail Mamiashvili also attended the session in a tremendous show of support for the sport. This was exactly the sort of exposure that Condron was hoping for when he took on the responsibilities of FILA Press officer just one month earlier.

Later that evening, Condron wrote about Lalovic's talk and the reactions that it brought. Some excerpts from his report...

To All

Today was pretty good for the sport of wrestling. Nenad did a hell of a job. He did the speech in English... we thought about changing to French, then Russian, but he was going strong and kept it in English.

... got him with L'Equipe today... and set up another with L'Equipe in two weeks before the Moscow Congress. And talked with Russians about media setup at Congress. Told them they had to have good media setup because that's where we change our lives. We want coverage and I'm recruiting here. Recruited AFP, Reuters, AP, and a few others for May.

...Lalovic was very happy with today's talk... got a good applause... and thanks from the AIPS Secretary General for "his heartfelt presentation." The slides were great and we added about 10 others from the Russians.

After Lalovic's talk a Ukrainian journalist got up to the mike and said AIPS should draft a document demanding the IOC get wrestling back in the Games. Everyone applauded... Lalovic said. "Thanks, we're trying to do things right and we appreciate your passion."

It went well today. Probably 100% support from these international journalists. He got about 10 followup media interviews after he finished. The Russians... wrestling federation, minister of sport, head of Sochi 2014... were totally great.

...this was a good day and it's still going on.

Bob

One week later, on the other side of the world, the 15th annual IOC Sport for All world conference took place in Lima. This conference was officially hosted by the IOC with an aim "to encourage and support the efforts of sharing health and social benefits to be gained by all members of society through regular physical activity." This initiative is based upon the Olympic charter, which says that "the practice of sport is a human right."

Dziedzic and Scherr were there representing international wrestling and the effort to Keep Olympic Wrestling.

For decades, wrestling had suffered from FILA's lack of interaction and camaraderie with the IOC at all levels. It undoubtedly had considerable catching up to do with the other sports prior to the coming election. Dziedzic and Scherr's job was to demonstrate that indeed FILA was changing from its aloof, arrogant style, while at the same time delivering the message of long-overdue change within the sport.

When not taking part in the scheduled meeting sessions during the week, Dziedzic and Scherr took the opportunity to introduce (or in some cases re-introduce) themselves to roughly 30 IOC members at the conference and discuss FILA's strategy and progress in making substantive changes to wrestling.

Their introduction of the idea that FILA develop a Sport for All Commission was applauded. Feedback indicated that the two delegates were well received and that positive messages about wrestling were getting out.

Both men were stunned to notice that wrestling's competition — squash, karate, baseball/softball, wakeboarding — were noticeably absent from the conference; perhaps they were unaware that it was an IOC election year and many candidates would be present.

As a postscript to the Lima trip, Dziedzic and Scherr were not the least disappointed when they heard the news on their way home that Major League Baseball Commissioner Bud Selig announced that baseball would not be able to change its schedule to allow major league players to compete in future Olympic Games.

CHAPTER 11 / **Fighting on Two Fronts**

I N APRIL, Nenad Lalovic announced that a special meeting (called the Extraordinary Congress) of the FILA national federations would take place on Saturday, May 18 in Moscow. That meeting would be preceded by a FILA Bureau session the prior afternoon and evening. The agenda would be brimming with hot topics — the final receipt of nominations and election of a permanent FILA President; the presentation of proposed 'new rules' for freestyle and Greco-Roman wrestling; discussions about FILA infrastructure changes; and an update to the membership about the all-important presentation to the IOC Executive Board just 12 days later.

With 24 members now on the FILA Bureau and numerous other interested parties from the 177 national federations, many opinions were being put forth regarding decisions that FILA should be making to improve the sport of wrestling and appease the IOC.

With just six weeks to go before the presentations to the IOC Executive Board, it was apparent that Lalovic and his supporters were fighting battles on two fronts — internally, with Raphy Martinetti's challenge against Lalovic for FILA President; and, externally, doing what needed to be done to win the IOC vote. Fortunately, for the most part, the outside world was well sheltered from the cunning, internal politics brewing amongst FILA Bureau members.

Martinetti could not help but promote his own agenda with his former Bureau constituents, as illustrated by this letter...

TO ALL FILA BUREAU MEMBERS
Dear Colleagues,
I decided to send you this letter after reading the last initiative of the Commit-

tee to Preserve Olympic Wrestling (CPOW) that was created by USA Wrestling to "enhance the worldwide strategy established by FILA and to ensure that wrestling remains as a core sport of the Olympic Games" (cf. article published on the FILA website on 25 March 2013).

I do not know if the Bureau was consulted on the decision to place the communication campaign in the sole hands of USA Wrestling, but it seems that the CPOW President, Bill Scherr, did not receive certain strategic information and operates against IOC's expectations.

In the article that was published on USA Wrestling's website on 10 April 2013 and re-published by PR Newswire on 11 April 2013, it is mentioned that CPOW called upon UFC, the biggest professional Mixed Martial Arts promotion, and its President, Dana White, for active support of the wrestling campaign.

The articles are available at the following links and in full in the enclosed documents: http://www.themat.com/section.php?section_id=3&page=showarticle&ArticleID=26323 http://www.prnewswire.com/news-releases/committee-to-preserve-olympic-wrestling-cpow-to-partner-with-ufc-and-mixed-martial-arts-202554051.html

As IOC has recently recommended FILA to remove amateur MMA from its sports because of the association that can be made with professional MMA that enjoys a dreadful reputation among the IOC members (violence, sexism, doping, etc.), CPOW does not find any better idea than ask for UFC's help in defending wrestling on the Olympic program.

Are the Bureau members conscious of backing a PR strategy that consists in shooting one's own foot?

Please be informed that I did not remain inactive since our meeting in Phuket. I conducted a thorough analysis of the wrestling rules that I am ready to share with the Bureau if you deem it useful.

Yours sincerely,
Raphaël Martinetti
Martigny, 12 April 2013

Stan Dziedzic was not standing for any of Martinetti's antics. He responded quickly...

Dear Raphy Martinetti,

I am dismayed and disappointed by your letter (dated 12 April, 2013) in which you insult the intellectual agility of my FILA Bureau colleagues and me by purporting; it was FILA's "decision to place the communication campaign in the sole hands of USA Wrestling." The Committee to Preserve Olympic Wrestling (CPOW) was formed to assist USA Wrestling in its efforts to keep wrestling as an Olympic sport. CPOW was never given authorization by FILA or its leaders regarding CPOW's contact with

MMA promotional companies nor did CPOW inform FILA of its actions. I trust your veiled attempt to misrepresent and undermine the efforts of a group committed to the preservation of our sport in the Olympic Program will fall on deaf ears among my FILA Bureau colleagues. I fully expect my colleagues at the next FILA Bureau meeting to unwind the direct connection you introduced with the violent Mixed Martial Arts (MMA).

Your suggestion that CPOW "operates against IOC'S expectation" is a mischaracterization. Even hinting that CPOW or FILA are recommending the introduction of striking or violence in wrestling is simply untrue. As I have conveyed to you many times, the concept of violence in wrestling escapes me. Wrestling's fundamental nature encourages its participants to appreciate one's opponent based on his or her character and will. Wrestling and violence are not compatible. Your proposition that the CPOW or by extension FILA are either advocating Olympic wrestling mutates into a MMA; or, that any form of violent striking be part of an Olympic sport is simply a fantasy. A designed delusion to promote your own agenda!

When you first chose to embrace MMA and place it under FILA's umbrella, I cautioned you to draw the line at violent striking. As you should have known, wrestlers are dedicated to developing skills which allow them to dominate yet never injure his or her opponent. Nonetheless, it cannot be denied, talented wrestlers — save the inherent violent component — embody many of the requisite physical attributes and technical skills required to succeed in what has been branded by some as Ultimate Fighting (UF). Most of the other combative Olympic sports — Judo, Taekwondo, Boxing to name a few — also provide talent to ultimate fighting.

Twisting any discussions CPOW may have had with the President of UFC Dana White to suggest a nefarious partnership was formed is disingenuous. Raphy, each of us has been given enormous trust by the worldwide wrestling community; yet now you seem intent on undermining that honor. As I stated in Phuket, I never questioned your intentions or commitment, but the current circumstances require different leadership. On behalf of all the aspiring wrestlers of the world, I urge to reconsider and see the fallacy of your quest to return to the FILA Bureau.

Sincerely,
Stan Dziedzic
FILA Vice President
CC: Fila Bureau, 16 April, 2013

Two weeks later, Martinetti's long-time ally, Matteo Pellicone, wrote a letter to each Bureau member giving his view on several issues facing the group as they prepared to meet the day before the Extraordinary Congress in Moscow. FILA was in the process of addressing a wide spectrum of intertwined controversial issues

regarding the wrestling competition. These included...
- New rules
- Increased opportunities for women wrestlers — number of weight classes and number of qualifiers; thus,
- Potentially fewer opportunities for male wrestlers — number of weight classes and number of qualifiers
  - Uncertain future of the Greco-Roman discipline
  - Potentially fewer wrestling medals awarded
  - Potentially fewer officials
  - Seeding
  - Weight classes wrestled over one or two days
  - Potentially less time/days of total wrestling competition

Dziedzic introduced Pellicone's letter with a memo of his own to several CPOW members and consultants. He pointed out that Pellicone was a long-standing member of FILA who was rumored to be Milan Ercegan's choice to replace him when the FILA membership instead elected Martinetti as their President in 2002. Dziedzic noted that Pellicone had broad support across the Bureau, and particularly appealed to those in the less advanced wrestling countries.

Dziedzic appeared dismayed, but not surprised, by Pellicone's most controversial suggestion to merge or unify the two styles of men's wrestling (freestyle and Greco-Roman). Apparently the two FILA Bureau vice-presidents discussed this topic last year at the Olympic Games in London, but Pellicone never offered a solution on how to accomplish this unification. Dziedzic saw this as an ongoing problem for FILA to work out.

Dziedzic also pointed out that his own desire to reduce the number of qualifiers per weight class rather than reducing the number of weight classes may not resonate well with Pellicone and a majority of the Bureau members. Many do not want to lose qualifiers because of their concern for those smaller national federations whose budgets are dependent upon the number of their wrestlers who indeed qualify for the Games.

Here is Pellicone's letter...

Dear Mr President, dear friends,

In a few days' time Congress will be called upon to decide on the strategies to adopt to get Wrestling back into the Olympic programme. I believe it is useful, in view of the short time available, to let you have the following considerations:

1) There is now a widely held belief that the decision made by the IOC Executive Committee was not based on an objective examination of different sporting disciplines, but the result of actions taken by pressure groups, facilitated by the secret ballot system;

2) We refuse to believe that Wrestling is in 26th place in the ranking of sporting disciplines examined by the IOC Executive Committee, based on parameters including: number of affiliated National Federations, number of active participants, nations present at Olympics, educational value of the discipline, media interest, television audience, etc. FILA is entitled to know the ranking of the 26 sports examined, with the relative scores for each parameter, and the IOC has the duty of making these results public to ensure the transparency and honour of its actions;

3) FILA did not feel threatened by the reduction in the number of main sports from 26 to 25, nor by sports such as Athletics, Boxing, Fencing, etc. The letter full of praise sent to the FILA President on 16/08/2012 by Mr Gilbert Felli (coordinator of the Olympic Programme Committee) and Mr Christophe Dubi (IOC Sports Director) amply corroborated this belief;

4) Culpably, absolutely no account was taken of the fact that Wrestling, together with very few other disciplines (athletics, boxing, pankration, etc.) had been part of the ancient Olympic Games for over a thousand years, and that the Olympics themselves have been spoilt by its being removed from the programme . The Olympic anthem, composed by Spiro Samara (text by Kostis Palamas), depicts the athlete "running, wrestling, throwing.....";

5) The decision of the Executive Committee was politically short-sighted, as it did not take into account the importance of wrestling for two of the three candidate cities for the 2020 Games: Tokyo and Istanbul;

6) At this moment in time the IOC is in difficulty, as it knows is has made a serious mistake. The reaction of public opinion worldwide has been very strong, and the IOC has been accused of putting commercial aspects first, and of not having the strength to counter lobbies;

7) It would have been useful, and necessary, after the Phuket meeting, to convene the Bureau at Corsier, at the end of March, to discuss and approve a strategy to defend our sport, which has been given a sound and unfair thrashing. But this was not done, and a valuable opportunity to come together to look at what we can do went to waste;

8) The proposal that came out of your talks with Mr Christophe Dubi was to eliminate the second bronze medal and to reduce the number of wrestlers able to qualify for the Olympics. I believe this is the worst of all possible solutions, as it would damage all National Federations, except for Russia and 4/5 other strong Federations. Many nations indeed would run the risk of having no wrestlers qualify for the Games, and this would then reduce the amount of financial resources available to them (through grants and sponsorships);

9) All combat sports (Boxing, with 13 weight categories, Judo, with 14 categories, and Taekwondo, with 8 categories) offer two bronze medals. Looking at the results from London, nations such as France, Turkey, Poland, Spain, Mongolia, Colombia, Lithu-

ania and the Democratic Republic of Korea would run the risk of obtaining no medals;

10) Proposals to change the rules that have been circulating up until now confirm the suspicions that there are few new ideas capable of making a difference, while we hear a lot of: "we have to modernise wrestling and make it more spectacular". The result being that over the past 20 years powerful members of the IOC have suggested eliminating one style of wrestling, causing harm to and indeed humiliating our sport, since they felt it was ridiculous to keep two such similar disciplines in the Olympic programme;

11) At this point in time I believe we should be asking President Rogge and the Executive Committee to propose to the IOC Session of Buenos Aires a recommendation to raise from 25 to 26 the number of main Olympic sports, and to raise from 28 to 29 the maximum number of disciplines to be included in the Olympic programme, at this moment just for 2020. If this decision were taken Wrestling would automatically be included in the Olympic programme;

12) To obtain this result it is necessary to offer something important to the IOC, so that it is able to modify its strategy. The only totally new way is to unify the two styles of Wrestling, with 8/10 weight categories for men and 6 for women;

13) The division into 6 weight categories for women is physiologically correct, as are the 8/10 categories for men. It should also be recalled that the women-men wrestlers ratio is 1to 10;

14) This would result in a halving of the number of judges present at the Games, and a reduction in the number of competition days. We believe however that the number of wrestlers qualifying for the Games should remain completely unchanged, increasing slightly the number of wrestlers in each weight category, and the four medals should also be kept on;

15) If it is developed with conviction and energy, such a proposal has a good chance of being accepted, and would be a long-term solution to the Wrestling "problem";

16) A single style of Wrestling would have the great advantage of being easier to promote, and easier to include in all multidisciplinary events. It would also be possible to channel all the financial resources of National Federations, which are quite scarce, towards its promotion;

17) To unify the two styles it would be necessary to base the discipline on Greco-Roman wrestling, adding to it the techniques of freestyle and, perhaps, the techniques of other styles of traditional or modern wrestling. It may be possible to create a commendable and highly spectacular style, which could continue to be called "Greco-Roman wrestling" or "Olympic Wrestling", or simply "Wrestling". The Wrestling of the ancient Greeks indeed did not have the limits that we have imposed on Greco-Roman;

18) The competition among combat sports is fierce, and in order to survive we

have to offer a forward-looking, high quality product, one that is firmly established in the Olympic programme. These are the two conditions for the survival of a sport that we love, and to which we have devoted so much of our time and energy.

Hope and trust that you will agree with the above, and am looking forward to meeting up with you in Moscow.

Matteo Pellicane
FILA Vice President
FIJLKAM President

Martinetti replied to Pellicone's letter, informing the Bureau that he was waiting for a decision from CAS (the Court of Arbitration for Sport) regarding his standing in FILA, that he basically supports Pellicone's recommendations and would like to see Beach Wrestling added to the Olympic wrestling program. His letter below was written in French, with an English translation following...

Mr. Matteo Pellicone,
To all Members of the Board,
Dear Matteo, dear friends,

It is with great pleasure that I finally receive an official letter from a member of the FILA Bureau. Since Mr. Lalovic has decided to boycott me, this letter is all the more important as it addresses the very real issues facing FILA. I never wanted to put myself forward because as you all know I brought a law to CAS (Court of Arbitration for Sport) in order to assert my rights in the face of those who organized a 'coup d'etat' for the sole purpose of controlling FILA.

Now that the case has been heard, both the Bureau and all National Federations will be informed of the decision to be taken by CAS in the next few days. The letter from Mr Pellicone directly addresses the IOC's decision, and had the group of conspirators been able to see beyond their own interest, I would have had the chance to tell you all about it in Phuket.

I hope that the CAS decision will give me the opportunity to work with you all on putting in place a strategy to save wrestling.

It seems to me that the current management has not consulted the Board on these matters, which are nevertheless more serious than any we have ever known. Similarly, the information we have been given is biased, and this is proven by the election results of CALA, which are still not posted on the site because unfavorable to Mr. Lavovic.

I personally agree with Mr. Pellicone's proposal for a new wrestling style, this resulting from the discussions that I have had with the directors of the IOC, before and after Phuket.

However, we must figure out how to avoid losing places for the wrestlers and not to lose medals. Reducing the number of referees is no problem at all, even though *according to the IOC, that is another topic altogether.*

According to my contacts a proposal of 7 men's categories of men, 7 women's categories and 4 categories of Beach Wretling (2 men's and 2 women's) would meet the approval of the IOC. With such a proposal we would be able to:
- *Achieve gender equality*
- *Keep the same number of medals.*
- *Keep the same number of participants.*
- *Bring something new to our program with the Beach while using the beach facilities.*

Here is, dear Matteo and dear friends of the Board, what we should have talked about, tested in competitions and made known to the IOC members in order to save wrestling.

All other actions to amend the rules and structure have nothing to do with the IOC's decision, and affect only the operation of FILA.

With my best regards to all.
Raphaël Martinetti

John Bardis weighs in with his thoughts on Martinetti and Dziedzic: "I have known of and witnessed Raphy's behavior and attitude for years and frankly I don't respect him. Martinetti is everything we teach our wrestlers not to be... he is arrogant, self-serving, undisciplined, lacks integrity and is a greedy slob. Stan is a disciplined, thoughtful, highly intelligent man who put his position and career at great risk for the benefit of our sport by offering his own resignation first. His years of credible relationships amongst the international wrestling community caused the FILA board to quickly reject his offer and do the right thing to oust Martinetti. This was a strong display of leadership by Stan and the catalyst for the removal of the worst sports executive in the modern Olympic movement.

"Stan has traveled the world for years doing his part for the betterment of wrestling, making enormous sacrifices of time and energy. His passion and love for the sport and its athletes has been his strength in overcoming criticism during these critical times. I'm glad he displayed the guts of the World Champion that he is... if Stan didn't step up we might well be out of the Olympic Games."

Dziedzic says of Martinetti: "We could write a whole book about him. It would be a horror story. Now going into the Moscow FILA Bureau meetings I don't think he has the support to take back the leadership role. Along the way he's been lying to everybody, 'Oh, I just want to help. I want to be on the Bureau so I can assist' when he really wanted to run again for President. If he gets back in, we'll have an even more difficult time in getting the IOC vote.

"It's a shame because his legacy would have been one of redefining the referee, instituting 'the challenge' which is a wonderful thing for the objectivity of the sport, holding the referees accountable, and so forth.

"However, when we had our FILA Rules Committee meetings we had so many false constraints put on us by Martinetti. For example — we had to stay with the best of three; or, the bout can't last more than six minutes. There were so many limitations even though at times we went outside of those limitations. We said, 'We can't make Greco interesting with what you have given us.' So we're going to suggest this and just argue it out.

"The FILA members were not happy with Martinetti but we would not have replaced him in Phuket if it had not been for the crisis that erupted. A number of people felt he was too authoritarian and autocratic in every sense and it was worsening. Even if we didn't know about how poorly the questionnaire was done, if not for the IOC recommendation, he'd still be in power right now.

"In Moscow, the questionnaire will be part of the argument not to have Martinetti back in power. I'll bring it up if no one else does. I don't know how he will build his case to resume leadership."

FILA caught a bit of a break when the IOC allowed the international federation a do-over on the questionnaire. Fed with raw data from Dziedzic, the Scherrs, USA Wrestling and others, Teneo Strategy took the first crack at redrafting the document. On April 12 Mike Coakley submitted Teneo's first draft to FILA.

Lalovic asked some key Bureau members to provide suggestions regarding the document, including a potential 6-6-6 weight class format, which may be necessary. Dziedzic, Mamiashvili and Fukuda emailed their suggestions to Lalovic by May 4. It is believed that the so-called final version of the document with the 6-6-6 proposal included was submitted the week ending April 19, but small modifications were made after subsequent discussions with key staff members.

Dziedzic says, "It's probably safe to say the final version of the IOC questionnaire was as close to a living, breathing document as any. After what most dubbed the final version was submitted, clarifications and adjustments were surely made up until the document prepared for the IOC Executive Board was finalized. FILA's new leaders were determined not to repeat mistakes made by its previous administration."

Even though FILA Bureau would not vote on the proposed 6-6-6 format until June, it was deemed necessary to submit the questionnaire well before then, with the caveat that FILA Bureau would need to ratify it.

CHAPTER 12 / Modernizing the Sport

INCREASING women's direct involvement with wrestling has been a painfully slow journey over the past 3,000 years. Until very recently wrestling has been a discriminating, hard-nosed, 'males only' club — practically forever. Women were not even allowed to watch the ancient Olympic Games, much less participate in them. Forty years ago virtually no girls wrestled in the United States high schools or colleges. Twenty years ago less than 800 girls wrestled in U.S. high schools. Only now has women's wrestling edged into the spotlight to the extent that gender equity was prominent on the list of issues that the IOC wanted FILA to consider improving as it fought to remain an Olympic sport.

From the historical perspective of women's freestyle Olympic wrestling, you have to go back and examine the 30-year tenure of Milan Ercegan as FILA President from 1972 to 2002. He is credited with revolutionizing wrestling by introducing female freestyle wrestling as a full-fledged discipline within FILA and the national federations.

The first FILA women's World championships took place in Lorenskog, Norway in 1987. France was the dominant team; their wrestlers won five of the nine contested weight classes. Women from Norway won three gold medals while the Japanese garnered a total of seven silver or bronze medals. Tricia Saunders won the USA's first World championship gold medal in women's freestyle competition in 1992 at 50kg.

It was not until the 2004 Games in Athens that women's freestyle wrestling made its Olympic debut. The women competed in just four weight classes, while the men competed in 14 — seven in freestyle, seven in Greco-Roman. Those 18 weight classes remained stable in the Olympics through the 2008 and 2012 Games. However, the weight classes are now being reconstructed to meet the social demands of the world — as well as the rising interest of women participating in the sport.

During the first dozen years of the 21st century, women's wrestling in the U.S. below the Olympic level has shown rapid growth. The number of girls wrestling in high school increased to more than 8,200 in 2011-12, according to the National Federation of State High School Associations. In addition, 22 U.S. colleges now sponsor a women's varsity wrestling program, even though the NCAA still does not recognize it as a sport.

Dziedzic adds his knowledge of the situation as he saw it during CPOW and FILA discussions taking place in the spring of 2013: "Last year in London, FILA had applied to add three women's weight classes to bring them up to seven. At the Bureau the number one priority item was obtaining more opportunities for the women wrestlers. The IOC gave us a counter-proposal to add two more women's weight classes if we would drop two men's weight classes — one in freestyle and one in Greco. We countered with the offer to reduce the number of men's qualifiers to equal the number of women's qualifiers.

"We thought that we would be successful since it was equal numbers but they did not agree to that. So we look back and say, 'Gee, did we make a mistake then?', asks Dziedzic. "It begins to send a message, right?

"That message being that it would be a lot easier if we could add another discipline — women's beach wrestling, for example. That would make two disciplines for the women and two disciplines for the men and we'd have seven weight classes each. However this is the time where the IOC is looking to reduce the numbers, so that really would not make sense."

In a letter sent in late April, Jim Scherr shared with some CPOW leaders the IOC's thinking on the gender equity and Greco issues...

".... one of the most important conversations was with C. Dubi (IOC Sports Director). *Of course we had quite a bit of interaction with him but he was specific this morning regarding gender equity and Greco-Roman. He indicated that the issue was not so much gender balance of numbers now with the EB (Executive Board), but it was the representation of women in the management of the sport, particularly the FILA Bureau. He indicated that the issue was Greco and that it wasn't well understood or regarded by the (EB) members. He indicated that if the women's Greco didn't exist, it shouldn't be artificially introduced on the programme. Stan mentioned beach wrestling but didn't seem to get much of a response...Greco will remain a serious issue with the membership."*

Dziedzic continues with his thoughts on the matter, "I would rather have a system of 7-7-7 weight classes and reduce the number of qualifiers. If I were doing the negotiating I would rather see 24 qualifiers in each of the women's weight classes and 12 for each of the men. We would then run four round-robins in each of the weight classes. Then the winners of the round-robins would advance into the semifinals and the losers would start to wrestle back.

"I understand the opposition to this since it is critical for some countries funding to have them qualify people for the Olympics and especially to gain medals. We certainly do not want to give up any medals. And that's why I don't want to give up any weight classes, either. In the 2016 Rio Olympics, I'm hoping we have 7-7-7 weight classes... 6-6-6 would be a fallback position," he said in April.

The 'elephant-in-the-room' during all this debate is the fact that there are two disciplines for men — freestyle and Greco-Roman — yet just the freestyle discipline for women. Women do not compete to any substantive extent in Greco-Roman wrestling worldwide. Many contend that this causes the IOC to sustain a concern about Greco-Roman wrestling. On the surface, it seems that since the IOC wants to limit the number of competitors in the Olympics, and more women wrestlers need to be added, then eliminating one of the two men's disciplines would be a potential solution.

Lalovic has mentioned on occasion that having FILA support Greco-Roman women's wrestling on the international level is not out of the question going forward.

Dziedzic chimes in, "I have a difficult time trying to make a decision between Greco and freestyle. The IOC is not going to make a decision for us. I would rather have it set up as, 'Okay, which style is the most exciting?' Then we have to make a decision as to whether we keep freestyle, or Greco, or some combination thereof. I don't know about a combination. How do you do that? Who is going to pull that rabbit out of the hat? Go one period for freestyle, then one period Greco? I doubt it.

"From my standpoint Greco has a very weak argument in this hemisphere. When you look back over the history of Olympic wrestling, we haven't medaled as much; there hasn't been as much interest in Greco. In this entire hemisphere, since the World championships were separated — one freestyle tournament, one separate Greco tournament — during the modern times when the Soviets entered, in roughly 20 years, the Championships were held in the Americas seven times. All in freestyle, none in Greco. Canada doesn't even sponsor a Greco-Roman team. That's telling.

"In Northern and parts of Continental Europe, Greco-Roman is more popular. Yet most of the Greco medalists competing in recent World championships have been from Eastern Europe and Russia. It would be a split and I don't know

U.S. Greco head coach Steve Fraser (left) is still ready to demonstrate proper techniques to his aspiring group of wrestlers.

how it would unfold. That's why I would rather say, 'Let's look at what transpires at Rio and evaluate that situation and go on from there and live with that number.'

"It's hard to sit here and say, 'I care about both equally.' It's a weak argument," Dziedzic concludes.

Naturally, those wrestlers and coaches specializing in the Greco-Roman style of wrestling believe differently. Writing in *USA Wrestler* magazine, U.S. National Greco-Roman coach Steve Fraser argues that wrestling should not be apologetic about supporting two separate disciplines, Greco-Roman and freestyle. They are both legitimate sports.

Fraser, an all-American wrestler at the University of Michigan and an Olympic Greco-Roman champion in 1984, goes on to write...

Greco has a great and wonderful history and has had many great champions like Alexander Karelin and Rulon Gardner (to name just two) which have provided icon superstars and thrilling matches for worldwide fans and children of the world to experience.

Greco is the ultimate hand-to-hand combat sport. The rich history of exciting and thrilling competitive battles among the thousands of fierce Greco-Roman warriors speaks for itself. And with the new rules being implemented, Greco will be extremely exciting; showcasing spectacular throws and maneuvers like it was in the 1970s and 1980s...

When we compare Greco to the other Olympic core sports we rank among the top in most all categories. Greco has about 180 countries that wrestle worldwide. Greco ticket sales sell out almost every Olympic Games. Greco Olympic television ratings are high. Greco is one of the most diverse sports when it comes to medals won by various countries.

There is a reason Greco-Roman wrestling has been in the Olympic Games from its beginnings back in 1896. It is because it is one of the purest, most physical competitive contests, with no weapons or teammates to assist. With the goal of defeating one's opponent by using mind, muscle, endurance and strategy — period!

The USA national team coach for the past 16 years concludes...

"Seven-seven-seven is the right thing to do for international wrestling. If the climate is not right for this now, we need to work on this goal for the future."

One of the other initial areas that FILA Bureau addressed was their own governance process. Feedback from the IOC Executive Board indicated that FILA should encourage more athletes and women to participate in having a voice in directing Bureau affairs.

The existing composition of the FILA Bureau includes no current athletes and two women out of the group of 24 Bureau members. For comparison sake, the IOC counts three females on their 15 member Executive Board. The FILA members added at the Phuket meeting in February were all males — Pedro Gama Filho, Alexander Karelin and Jim Scherr.

Dziedzic gave his account of the progress being made in this area prior to FILA's Extraordinary Congress summit in May: "Looking at the composition of the Bureau I don't think that there will be much opposition to improving women's rights within FILA. By the end of the weekend meetings in Moscow we will have in place a program for both the new Women's Commission and more representation for athletes on the FILA Bureau. I don't know how many of those positions will be filled but it will be substantial enough. It will be an evolutionary process. Women's rights vary all over the world — for instance women cannot wrestle in Iran... yet.

"I have already spoken to two female athletes [Carol Huynh and Lise Legrand

MODERNIZING THE SPORT 77

When competitors like Harry Lester and Ellis Coleman square off in a Greco-Roman match expect some high-flying moves. Tony Rotundo/WrestlersAreWarriors

who are participating in the St. Petersburg presentation to the IOC. I am encouraging them to run. They are both very active; their stories are interesting. One of them [Legrand] will be going to the IOC athletes commission in Singapore in June. They have both won an Olympic medal and they have excellent language skills. I would expect that they would come on to the FILA Bureau at the World championships in Budapest in September or at the latest at the FILA Extraordinary meeting in 2014. We will then initiate the Women's Commission. And we will also start a Sports for All Commission."

Dziedzic bring up a valid point about having current athletes competing and serving as active Bureau members, "Bringing a current athlete onto the Bureau gets a little tricky since we usually conduct our meetings during the World championships or the Olympics. Let's say FILA elected Jordan Burroughs to the group. Well, I don't think Burroughs, or any other competitor for that matter, would be concentrating on doing anything other than preparing for the competition. So, we expanded the 'athlete' definition to someone who has competed at a high level during the past four or five years. The IOC seems to be okay with this."

CHAPTER 13 / **Love Letters**

IN A VEILED attempt to derail wrestling's efforts, deposed FILA leader Raphy Martinetti composed and sent a letter to each FILA Bureau members dated May 11. In an apparent change of heart — read self-interest — he indicated that despite tendering his resignation at the Phuket FILA meeting after suffering a vote of no-confidence, he still should have been considered a member of the FILA Bureau. He also stated he disagreed with both the approach the FILA Bureau was taking and its planned presentation to the IOC Executive Board at its meeting at the end of May. The wounded yet unrepentant Martinetti intended to oppose Nenad Lalovic for the presidency of FILA. He put everyone on notice — he was not gracefully retiring, no matter how damaging it would have been to the sport of wrestling.

TO ALL FILA BUREAU MEMBERS
Dear Colleagues,

On 10 May 2013, CAS (Court of Arbitration for Sport) ruled on the appeal I lodged in order to have my rights respected in front of Mr. Lalovic's arbitrary and abusive actions following the Bureau meeting in Phuket.

CAS confirmed what I had always claimed: my resignation from the FILA presidency did not end my term as FILA Bureau member, which I hold until September 2014. It is now clear that Mr. Lalovic's moves to exclude me from the Bureau had only one purpose: to make sure he would remain the only candidate to the FILA presidency.

CAS however confirmed Mr. Lalovic's nomination and the organization of the extraordinary congress in Moscow, although they were both conducted in total violation of the FILA Constitution, but I respect CAS' decisions.

On the occasion of this congress, we must focus on the most important and urgent matters, that is: the strategy, means, and financial commitments necessary to maintain wrestling on the Olympic program. The FILA Bureau and National Federations must remain the main stakeholders of these actions and not external agents.

In my capacity as Bureau member, I protest against the items that will be submitted to the congress' approval, because the process was violated both the Constitution and Bureau members and National Federations' rights. The agenda notably provides for:

a) Amendment of the Statutes

That item cannot be discussed during the congress, because, to my knowledge, the Bureau members and National Federations did not receive the necessary documents in advance. No explanation can justify the proposed amendments.

b) Amendment of the Wrestling Rules

The Bureau and National Federations did not receive the documents either and no test event took place to assess the modifications' effects. Until now, all proposals came from people who did not advocate for the global benefit of wrestling, but for national interests.

c) Election of Mr. Lalovic to the presidency

If we consider that Mr. Lalovic was elected acting President in Phuket, there is no obligation to have his mandate confirmed in front of an extraordinary congress, especially if we consider that by 8 May, only 6 Oceania countries, 4 European countries, 5 American countries, 2 Asian countries, and 2 African countries (that is 21 countries) had confirmed their flights to Moscow.

According to the Constitution, the candidacies to the FILA presidency must be sent 3 months before the congress, but that obligation was not respected for Moscow. It is therefore imperative that the Bureau decides to hold the elective extraordinary congress on the occasion of the World Championship in Budapest.

I ask Mr. Lalovic that these three topics be voted during the Bureau meeting in Moscow before being submitted to the congress. Be informed that I will attend the Bureau meeting to defend the Constitution and the Bureau members and National Federations' interests.

I also note that the minutes of the Bureau meeting in Phuket mentioned that the status of the 3 co-opted members was to be discussed on the occasion of the next Bureau meeting. Since this item does not appear on the agenda of the Moscow meeting, I consider that we will not discuss it and leave it aside until the next meeting.

I look forward to meeting you soon. Sincerely yours,
Raphaël Martinetti
Président FILA
FILA Bureau member
Martigny, 11 May 2013

Zamel Al-Shahrani, FILA Bureau member from Qatar, warned other Bureau members about supporting Raphy Martinetti's quest to return as FILA President.

Needless to say, Martinetti's letter, replete with self-serving accusations and innuendos, did not go over well with many of his fellow Bureau members. The odds were stacked against him, though. Many believed that if Martinetti regained control, the IOC would never seriously consider keeping wrestling in the Olympics. One of the newly-elected Bureau members, Zamel Al-Shahrani of Qatar, wrote a letter to all FILA Bureau members denouncing Martinetti's quest for the Presidency...

To: FILA Bureau Members
Subject: Reproducing failure
Dear Colleagues,
I will not talk about the crisis that we are facing now with IOC because we all know what is going on and the new leadership of FILA is doing well to get out of this crisis with less damage to our Wrestling sport.
I will talk to you about other subject that I believe it is worse than the crisis that we face right now, there are (signals/attempts) from some of us and other self-interested to reproduce the ex-leadership which failed to do the changing and development that IOC was talking about for many years... and failed to anticipate what would happened to our sport in future.

Dear Colleagues, if we allowed this to happened it well lead to the destruction of the FILA Bureau members reputation and the future of wrestling... because this simply means that we do not have vision and alternative options to solve our problems and lead this International organization to save side.

I have nothing against Mr. Martinetti in person, but I judge him in the way he was running FILA in the past and the way he is behaving now, Mr. Martinetti is not the right person to lead our Wrestling sport in this difficult time. We need a new face and the world also wanted to see a new leadership for the Wrestling sport.

Please do not reproduce failure leadership.

I said that — with full responsibility and peaceful conscience.

Recently I have seen the ugly face of sport, I saw people have been driven to do things that they do not know why they are doing it. You and me do not want to see this happen in our sport anymore. We do not want to see this in our extraordinary meetings in Moscow. Let us stop deceiving people for self-interest. Stop this absurd.

If we really care and are sincere about our sport, we must united behind the acting president Mr. Lalovic and help him to make the changing that we all talking about.

For our acting president... we wanted to see a new vision and new concrete strategy for our sport.

FILA members remember this... we will be witnessed and judged by history.

See you in Moscow.

Zamel Al-Shahrani

FILA member

CHAPTER 14 / New York, New York

WRESTLING federations worldwide agreed — FILA should officially declare May World Wrestling Month. And it did, as suggested by the consultants at KOM. As events materialized, it was becoming clear that May 13-19 was unofficially World Wrestling Week. And what a week it was!

As the week approached, the wrestling world anxiously awaited a jam-packed six days. USA Wrestling scheduled a Tuesday press conference and luncheon at the home of the United Nations. On Wednesday, the New York City based Beat-the-Streets organization would host an exhibition match dubbed Rumble on the Rails between the best wrestlers in the U.S. and the national teams from Iran and Russia at the world-famous Grand Central Station in Manhattan. CPOW and USA Wrestling would tout these matches as the sport's centerpiece event of the month, demonstrating wrestling's unique ability to bring harmony to an unlikely alliance of world powers.

FILA scheduled a Bureau meeting on Friday and an Extraordinary Congress session of its 177members on Saturday in Moscow, Russia. These assemblies would mold and reveal the cornerstone of FILA's proposed changes to keep wrestling in the Olympics. And, the Los Angeles-based Beat-the-Streets group organized a wrestling match on Sunday afternoon between the USA and Iran in Southern California.

Lalovic arrived in New York City to meet with the press regarding Iran, Russia and the United States joining in an unprecedented axis-of-power platform that underlined FILA's plans for keeping wrestling as part of the Olympics. He also seized the opportunity to oversee the pageantry and competition in the Rumble on the Rails wrestling matches scheduled for Wednesday, May 15. Reportedly, 186 credentialed media from all the major agencies were there.

Irony was not lost on the event planners for Tuesday's invitation-only press conference luncheon. The setting — the landmark United Nations Building overlooking the city's East River. Among the first to congregate around the white linen-clothed luncheon tables were the national wrestling teams from Iran, Russia and the USA. The *real* UN, the uniting of nations for a common cause, was on full display.

With USA Wrestling's Gary Abbott serving as moderator, Lalovic opened the session with a cordial welcome to all. Speaking fluent English from the podium, he proclaimed that FILA would soon be endorsing a New Vision concept for wrestling so that the 30 million wrestlers worldwide who work out and compete on a regular basis could continue to keep their Olympic dreams alive.

Other wrestling leaders — from USA Wrestling, CPOW, Beat-the Streets and the coaching staffs of the three competing nations — followed with much the same message: "Wrestling deserves to be a core Olympic sport. We are doing everything we can to keep it that way. We are taking this as an opportunity to make substantive changes to improve our sport but we need the continued help of everyone connected with wrestling to do their part."

Among those speaking from the dais that day was actor Billy Baldwin. Several years ago he played a significant role in helping prevent his alma mater, Binghamton University, from dropping wrestling at the NCAA Division I level.

Baldwin praised wrestling for what it had accomplished that day at the UN. "Today, wrestling was able to do at the UN what every sitting President from Obama to Jack Kennedy has been unable to do — that's bringing the United States, Russia and Iran to the table, on the same page, with a united voice working toward the same goals and objectives. Wrestling was able to do this very quickly and in an impressive fashion, and I'm very proud of that."

The crowning moment of the day was the mock 'fighting-weight weigh-in' conducted by Abbott and CPOW's Wes Battle. Each contestant and his opponent, dressed in their street clothes, met at the front of the room, stepped on the scale, had their weight announced, shook hands with each other, and, for the paparazzi, gave a mighty flex and flashed a mild smile. It was feelgood time — something those unfamiliar with the sport of wrestling may find astonishing for such an intensely competitive event.

The press corps hovered around the wrestling bigwigs in attendance — Bill Scherr, Stan Dziedzic, Rich Bender, Jordan Burroughs, Kyle Dake, Mike Novogratz, Billy Baldwin, the team coaches and wrestlers — but Lalovic's pres-

Actor Billy Baldwin, a former high school and college wrestler in New York, spoke eloquently about the magic of bringing the U.S, Russia and Iran together in New York City. Tony Rotundo/WrestlersAreWarriors

Dan Gable meets up with Beat-the Streets New York President Mike Novogratz in their combined effort to save Olympic wrestling. Danielle Hobeika

ence was undoubtedly the main attraction. Reporters and photographers from *Sports Illustrated*, *USA Today*, *The New York Times*, Flowrestling and many others (including several foreign correspondents) were all vying for his precious time and words. The burly Serbian did not disappoint. Within 24 hours the mainstream media were reporting story after story of wrestling's fight to survive as an Olympic sport.

In his interview with *Sports Illustrated*, Lalovic revealed some of the problems that wrestling faced during the past years: "We had a president who had a telephone line to the referees. They were always under pressure because he was phoning in to them. Can you imagine that? Can you imagine Sepp Blatter [soccer's president of FIFA] phoning to say that play was offside? I believe the IOC started to be very attentive to us after the scandal in 2008 when the Swedish wrestler did not want to receive his medal."

Lalovic also commented that he thought the greatest potential for growth in wrestling was in Africa, where recently in Dakar 60,000 people came to watch a wrestling match. He concluded his remarks by saying that FILA would consider

Maryland native Helen Maroulis won her match in Grand Central Terminal — by fall over her Russian opponent. John Sachs

Recent Cornell graduate Kyle Dake won his international debut over his opponent from Iran in the Beat-the-Streets dual meet. John Sachs

holding future wrestling matches in other non-traditional venues, such as "an old Roman arena." Lalovic was prophetic. Less than two months later, FILA would sponsor an international wrestling tournament at the site of the birthplace of the Olympic movement — the hallowed grounds in Olympia, Greece.

Lalovic appeared jovial in front of the crowd and cameras. Yet he likely had some apprehension internally. It is not easy to successfully pull off a highly promoted and visible event with three distinct purposes. But that was the challenge facing him and the organizers of New York City's Rumble on the Rails.

First of all, this wrestling extravaganza — and the gala party afterwards — represented the annual fundraiser for the City's Beat-the-Streets organization. In past years the event was held on an aircraft carrier parked on New York's riverfront, twice in Times Square, and now this year in Grand Central Station's iconic Vanderbilt Hall. Once again it was expected to raise over $1 million for the nonprofit group.

Secondly, it was billed as a marquee event to show the world, particularly those IOC members paying attention, that wrestling indeed is a special sport that brings together disparate nations and attracts international attention. Thirdly, it was a competition between three of the premier wrestling countries in the world. The matches may have been labeled an exhibition, but among wrestlers there is no such thing. The matchups were compelling and competitive. No one wanted to be embarrassed, particularly the competitors.

The Beat-the-Streets people took a gamble with their venue. Vanderbilt Hall holds only 700 or so spectators. In order to meet their budget, they needed to set a high ticket price, and they did: $1,000 for the U.S. wrestling matches against Iran and Russia, along with entry into the evening party. For just $250 one could attend the U.S.-Russia match and the gala. They sold out. Mr. Novogratz reaffirmed that he knows how to raise money!

Those fortunate enough to be inside Vanderbilt Hall on Wednesday, May 15 will attest to the magical trappings of this 100-year-old relic. Never before in the United States has an amateur wrestling match been contested inside a makeshift arena dripping with so much exposed marble and gilded chandeliers.

In the absence of smoke and mirrors, ringside announcer Noel Thompson, sporting dark shades and tuxedo, added to the Greatest Show on Earth atmosphere with his introductions resembling the Thriller in Manila. Working in a seamless partnership with Thompson was mega-promoter Scott Casber, who introduced and interviewed the wrestlers, coaches, fans and celebrities between the matches.

Stars such as Dan Gable, Kurt Angle, Cael Sanderson, Billy Baldwin, Mike Golic, Ronnie Lott, Mark Ruffalo and Reza Razavi all helped to turn Vanderbilt

Hall into a tangible example of the sport's ability to bridge cultural and ideological boundaries. Casber recognized that, saying, "This was the beginning of one of the greatest PR efforts the world of sport has ever known."

Months later Rumble on the Rails was nominated for Best Amateur Sporting Event for the 2013 Sports Travel Awards.

The organizers' smartest play was obtaining live television rights to the matches. Both of the dual meets were broadcast live on national television, with the USA vs. Iran match on NBC Sports Channel, and the USA vs. Russia match on Universal Sports. Those fans whose bank accounts didn't afford them the opportunity to attend in person, or those who lived too distant from the metro New York City area, could flick on their television sets and watch the competition live from their living rooms or office buildings.

The freestyle competition mesmerized the crowd, particularly the jubilant Iranian fans. Although the Iranians won by a dominating team score of 6-1 over the USA, and Russia fell by 7-1 to the Americans, the individual matches were close and highly competitive. The USA 74kg freestyle grapplers were the host-country heroes as Jordan Burroughs, Kyle Dake and David Taylor all handily won their respective matches. In the lone women's match, Helen Maroulis thrilled the crowd when she pinned her Russian opponent. Those victories, plus the spectacular one by Logan Stieber over the #1 ranked wrestler in the world at 60kg, Russia's Opan Sat, overshadowed some criticism about the lack of activity and scoring in the three Greco-Roman events.

Everything appeared to go well — until the day after the matches, Thursday, May 16. IOC member Anita DeFrantz from the United States wrote a damning HuffPost internet sports blog. The headline screamed, 'Wrestling Needs to Get a Grip!' Speaking bluntly, the author condemned FILA for promoting a wrestling event that featured "16 contests — 15 for men, 1 for women." She went on, "Seriously guys? This is what happens when women are excluded from leadership positions."

It was a tough blow to take given the timing and the circumstances regarding the gender equity issue lingering between FILA and the IOC. Not surprisingly, the wrestling community became defensive, arguing that Beat-the-Streets is the acknowledged leader in promoting girls' wrestling opportunities in urban areas across the U.S.

But the damage had been written.

One can argue the point that this gender issue was not really the fault of the USA organizers. Due to religious beliefs, the Iranians do not permit women to wrestle. When the organizers agreed to have the Russians participate, they asked the Russians to bring athletes in all three styles. The composition of the Russian team came from them. Often with the Russians their teams are determined by the ability to obtain visas in time, as well as the status of their training. Evidently they could only muster one female competitor.

And then came another apparent setback — the Iranians declared that they must return to Iran and could not participate in the Los Angeles United 4 Wrestling event set for Sunday, May 19.

Thompson recalls, "The Iranian team leader came to us the morning after the Grand Central matches, saying, with fear in his eyes, 'We have to go home. Our government in Tehran is demanding that we leave here immediately.' I tried to talk him out of it. He was insistent in telling us, 'You have to let us go. You don't understand. I have to go back home. These are orders from the top.'

"We realized we had no choice. Consequently, all afternoon, all evening, until 2am, along with Rich Bender, Pete Isias, Mitch Hull, Terry Steiner and others, we scrambled to save the Sunday afternoon engagement in L.A. — scheduled a mere three days away."

The diligence of wrestling's leadership and the camaraderie of the worldwide wrestling community paid off. The men asked the Russians if they would extend their stay in the U.S. and immediately fly to Los Angeles to wrestle another set of freestyle and Greco-Roman matches on Sunday. They accepted. A call went out to the Canadians asking if their women's team would, on a moment's notice, assemble in Los Angeles to wrestle against the U.S. women freestylers. Miraculously, they graciously accepted the offer.

"It was then that I realized that I needed to be there in Los Angeles for Sunday's festivities," said Thompson. "I had helped Andy [Barth] establish the Beat-the-Streets Los Angeles organization just one year ago. I wasn't planning on attending but Andy was encouraging me to serve as the Master of Ceremonies. I couldn't say 'no' to him. I bought a plane ticket, grabbed my tuxedo and dark shades, and headed for the west coast. I was very excited."

CHAPTER 15 / **Moscow... A Turning Point**

AS THE matches were wrapping up and the wrestling fans were celebrating at the Beat-the-Streets evening gala in New York City, several members of FILA and USA Wrestling were preparing to fly to Moscow. Once there, the schedule called for a FILA Bureau meeting on Friday afternoon and evening, May 17, leading up to the FILA Extraordinary Congress session with national federation delegates set for Saturday — and a potential showdown between Nenad Lalovic and Raphy Martinetti.

At stake was the leadership reigns to fill the unexpired term — until September 2014 — of FILA President.

Friday morning, just prior to the FILA Bureau meetings, Lalovic called a meeting of the FILA Executive Committee. Coincidentally it was reported, both Messrs Ayik of Turkey and Dziedzic of the USA mused that, since being appointed Vice-Presidents three years earlier, neither had ever been invited to such a meeting.

Lalovic wanted to discuss with his Vice-Presidents the proposed sequence of events on the Friday meeting agenda. He was not pleased with what he saw as a tactical move by Martinetti supporters to restore the deposed President to office. He asked the Executive Committee to approve a Bureau agenda modification whereby a review of the nominations received for the election of the FILA President be placed at the start of the meeting rather than towards the end. The Executive Committee agreed to support this strategic change.

At the Friday afternoon Bureau meeting at Moscow's Hotel Metropol, Lalovic asked the Bureau members to approve the reshuffled agenda. Martinetti announced that he disagreed with this proposal. Lalovic called for a vote on his agenda modification. Twelve Bureau members agree to modify the agenda per

Nenad Lalovic won the vote for FILA President at the Extraordinary Congress meeting by a landslide.

Matteo Pellicone, FILA Vice-President and President of Italy's FIJLKAM Federation, came to Lalovic's defense in Moscow.

Lalovic's request, with just one vote against. The process of taking nominations for the Presidency would preceed all other business items.

Many questioned the logic of moving the election of the President before confirming the voting rights of the three new co-opted FILA Bureau members — Fihlo, Karelin and Scherr — all of whom supported Lalovic. When asked, Dziedzic conceded, "I was unsure, since in Phuket several committee members supported Martinetti. But Lalovic's instincts proved correct." Yet not before some spirited debate with 'friends-of-Martinetti' as they were referred to.

At this juncture, it was Italy's Mateo Pellicone who emerged as a key player in the intrigue. It appears that he was beginning to discern the flaws in his long-time friend in the Bureau, Martinetti. Rumors persisted that one of Italy's IOC members was educating Pellicone. On the other hand perhaps he was impressed with Lalovic's leadership style and the progress that FILA had made since Phuket. When Pellicone courageously proclaimed to the Bureau members, "We must all stand behind President Lalovic if wrestling is going to survive," it was all but over for Martinetti's reelection chances.

Eventually, lacking support from even his long-time confidantes, Martinetti withdrew his candidacy. Although Dziedzic would neither confirm nor deny it, apparently Martinetti dispensed of pre-planned arguments to postpone most of the changes until the World Championship in Budapest in September. He must have seen the writing on the wall and the lack of votes sitting around the table. The campaign to Save Olympic Wrestling was still alive.

Trying to protect his legacy, Martinetti was vocal in his staunch belief that the IOC would not overturn their February recommendation and vote in favor of Olympic wrestling at the upcoming St. Petersburg session. Reportedly, he suggested to other Bureau members that FILA was wasting its time even going to St. Petersburg. Jim Scherr recalls, "He was adamant and arrogant in the certainty of his belief to the point of being insulting, and questioning my knowledge of the IOC and its workings."

Once Martinetti announced that he was not going to run for the Presidency, normalcy returned, if ever a FILA Bureau meeting could be referred to as normal. Among the key discussions and decisions made by the Bureau on Friday included...

- The nomination of Lalovic for approval as President by members attending the Extraordinary Congress meeting the following day.
- Report on the actions taken by FILA for the reintegration of wrestling in the 2020 Games.
- Discussion of the following day's presentation of a new FILA Constitution which would include provision for greater representation within wrestling for women and athletes.
- Discussion and final formulation of a proposal to be presented for approval the following day on changes to wrestling rules in both freestyle and Greco-Roman competition.

FILA, as approved by the Bureau in Phuket, had offered to fly one delegate from each of FILA's 177-member countries to the association's Extraordinary Congress meeting on Saturday — 111 showed up, plus 22 Bureau members. "We want to bring in more countries. It's important to show that we care about our sport and the countries that practice wrestling," Lalovic announced.

It was also very important that the Moscow meeting receive the maximum media coverage possible. Press Chief Bob Condron explains, "I believed that it was critical that the media be on hand to see and report on the new look of FILA and wrestling. That is how we'd begin getting our message across to the IOC. I told Lalovic that we have to get the media there, even if a shit-storm occurs [read, if Martinetti and his cronies cause a scene]."

Condron prevailed. More than 100 media representatives were indeed on hand to cover both the Friday and Saturday sessions. That number included the three largest newspapers in the world, plus 10 television networks.

Condron concludes, "The stations sent out their broadcasts to approximately

50 million viewers. Interviews were streamed live from the hotel. The Russians jumped right in and did a great job. This day was a turning point in our campaign to reverse the IOC recommendation. I believed that it's what the media can do for you if you give them good access. We did and it worked!"

Mikhail Mamiashvili served as host for Saturday's Extraordinary Congress meeting at the Ritz-Carlton hotel in Moscow. He welcomed all delegates, explaining that the Bureau was doing everything possible to solve FILA's problems yet the Congress had frontline responsibility and must make wise decisions this day. Mamiashvili was followed to the podium by Vitaly Mutko, Russia Minister of Sports; Alexander Zhukov, President of the Russian Olympic Committee; Alexey Vorobiev, Moscow Sports Minister; and Vitaly Smirnov, President of Honour of the Russian Olympic Committee. All the speakers extend a warm welcome to the delegates, expressing optimism about wrestling's Olympic future.

Lalovic opened the FILA Congress meeting with a symbolic gesture. As delegates took their place in the conference room, they each found a sealed envelope at their assigned spot. The Serbian leader told them that they would soon come face-to-face with an important person in the historic undertaking of saving wrestling as an Olympic sport. As each delegate opened his or her envelope and found a mirror inside, Lalovic's message became clear — each one of them *was* 'the important person'. Each one needed to be an agent of change and their individual efforts on behalf of wrestling could make the difference between being in or out of the Olympics.

Lalovic stressed the importance of the meeting and the necessity of Congress making wise decisions regarding the FILA Constitution, new wrestling rules and FILA governance. He lauded two outside professional firms assisting FILA in getting back its place in the Olympic Games — Teneo Strategy and TSE Consulting, both of whom were helping FILA with the preparation of its upcoming presentation in St. Petersburg.

A director of TSE Consulting, Lars Haue-Pedersen, addressed the group, noting that action on two fronts must be made simultaneously: public relations and lobbying of the IOC; and improvement and reinforcement of wrestling and its organization. He outlined key points for a worldwide wrestling strategic plan which would be developed in the coming months and presented during the World Championships in Budapest in September.

A copy of the FILA Constitution with the proposed new amendments was distributed beforehand to all national federations for their review. Since no delegate asked for an article-by-article review of the document, the Congress adopted globally the new Constitution without further remarks.

As part of the new Constitution at least one woman would become a FILA Vice-President. The new FILA Bureau would have 19 elected members, including three seats reserved for women and three seats reserved for recent Olympic and/or World champions. It would comprise 15 different commissions, including some new commissions and a restructuring of some of the existing commissions. Among the new commissions were the Women and Sport Commission and a Sport for All Commission. The Athletes Commission would be expanded and revised, providing more input from athletes in the FILA decision-making process.

Upon adoption of the new Constitution, Vice-President Dziedzic presented the proposals for the new rules which had been already sent to the federations. He emphasized that for practical reasons the Bureau did not approve the new rules line by line; instead the main changes constituted a foundation on which the rules may still evolve.

Highlights included...

• A match is divided into two three-minute periods. Scoring will be cumulative over the length of the match. A takedown is worth two points, making it more valuable than a point for the push-out or a penalty point. A seven-point difference in score will result in a technical fall. A five-point move or two three-point moves by a wrestler will result in a technical fall.

• In freestyle, the first passivity call will be a verbal warning. In the second instance of a passivity call, a 30-second clock will begin. If no athlete scores in those 30 seconds, a caution and a point will be awarded to the opponent of the passive athlete. In addition, if no athlete scores in the first two minutes of a period, referees must select one of the wrestlers as passive. In this situation, the passive wrestler must score within 30 seconds or the opponent receives a point.

The group deliberated at length when to implement the changes. They ultimately decided to initiate them immediately.

Lastly, it was time for the election of the FILA President. The election of nominee Nenad Lalovic was carried out by secret ballot. Of the 132 valid voters, 125 voted for Lalovic, with 7 'no' or 'absent' votes. He will serve out the term as FILA President until the next election at the 2014 Congress.

Left out of the debate and discussion was the important decision on how many weight classes would be proposed to the IOC for competition in future Olympic Games. Nor were the related issues of the number of Olympic qualifiers per style, medals awarded, officials needed and days of competition decided upon. Seeding or at least the separation of returning athletes from the previous World Championships was tabled. Bureau members voiced their opinion that eventually the two top two athletes or as many as four athletes would be placed in different brackets.

Measures of Titanic proportions had been accomplished during the two days in Moscow. The leaders would take the essence of the changes and present them to the IOC Executive Board in two weeks in St. Petersburg. Still, some cross words were reportedly exchanged amongst the Bureau members.

The RIA Novosti news agency reported in an article of 20 May: "Recriminations over wrestling's exclusion from the Olympics re-emerged Monday, as supporters of the sport's former chief (Raphy Martinetti) were accused of hurling insults at an official meeting. 'The meeting started with insulting words,' said Mikhail Mamiashvili, head of the Russian Wrestling Federation and seen as an ally of (newly elected President) Lalovic. 'It's a cause for serious investigation.'"

Speaking at a news conference, Mamiashvili said Martinetti and his supporters had accused the new regime of forcing through changes undemocratically, which Mamiashvili called "untrue and a lie." Martinetti stood for election alongside Lalovic for the president's job, but pulled out before the vote in an apparent show of reconciliation that Mamiashvili said was as significant as announcing he would not try to unseat Russian President Vladimir Putin.

"He understood he had zero chance, and then he retracted his candidature," the Russian said. "With the same level of seriousness, I could say that I am also retracting my candidature from the election to be president of the Russian Federation."

Mamiashvili rarely missed an opportunity to remind the deposed FILA president of his shortcomings. He reminded Martinetti about the Denmark World Championships several years ago, reportedly telling him, "The wrestlers had no food, and in some cases had to travel 50 kilometers and you proclaimed that it was an excellent competition. Nonsense! You took a sauna in the morning, gave out flowers at the ceremonies and then drank yourself to sleep. Of course it was a great World Championships for you; but not for the wrestlers."

CHAPTER 16 / Los Angeles... Without the Iranians

IT APPEARS as though only the Iranians really know exactly why they suddenly abandoned their plans to wrestle the USA team in Los Angeles and went home instead. Rumors circulated about unrest back in Iran due to upcoming national elections and possible protests in Los Angeles. The Iranians had a history of backing out of previous commitments. Some were even whispering and wondering if they ever really intended to go to the West Coast. One can only wonder.

The L.A. event, tabbed United 4 Wrestling, was just 72 hours away when the Iranians backed out. Thousands of tickets had been sold — and suddenly there was no opponent for the Americans to compete against. Beat-the-Streets Los Angeles leader Andy Barth recalls the drama: "The day that Iran decided not to come, I was actually flying back to Los Angeles from New York. I had arranged a charter to go from New York City to Stillwater to L.A. I was with my family and a few of the New York group. We were picking up another group of wrestlers who train at Oklahoma State and who wrestle for Titan Mercury in Stillwater. It was on that stopover that I first heard the news.

"At that point, the issue was still in doubt and there were several people like Rich Bender, Noel Thompson and Mo Tavakolian still working feverishly to prevent the Iranians from leaving. When we took off from Stillwater, we still were not sure but we started a process to make sure that we would have a conference call that night to assess the situation and see what we could do.

"Having said that, my gut feeling was that this was terrible; we could not recover and would have to cancel. I didn't know what the status of the Russians was or if we could get them to L.A. in time. I started to think about what other

Andy Barth successfully kept the United 4 Wrestling affair alive even though the Iranian wrestling team went home from their visit to America early.

international wrestlers we had training in the U.S. and could we get them to L.A. Also, were any other teams in close proximity? I was also concerned about whether our sponsors would continue their financial support. I thought if they stay in, there was a chance that we can pull something off. But it was going to take a lot of hard work on Thursday night to get a plan together."

On the Thursday evening conference call, Barth had to inform the event sponsor, the Semnani Family Foundation, about the change of plans. The Foundation is an international humanitarian organization based in Salt Lake City and founded by Khosrow Semnani, a prominent Iranian-American philanthropist.

Barth remembers the Semnani's generous reaction: "When we connected on the conference call that night, the unwavering support of the Semnanis sealed the deal. Khos was clear and firm in his comments that the Semnani Family

Foundation would continue with their financial support for this event. Various people, like Zeke Jones and Pete Isais, had been working their contacts around the wrestling community to start pulling together a new program and it looked like we would be able to bring a world class event to Los Angeles."

Barth and his associates let the significant local Iranian community know that their favorite sports team would not be coming to Los Angeles on Sunday after all — and offered ticket refunds to everyone. There was financial pain — USA Wrestling now had to pay the transportation and housing of the Russian and Canadian competitors. It was reported that 8,000 tickets were originally sold for the USA-Iran match; the final tally to watch the Americans wrestle the Russians and Canadians was more like 3,500 — still a good number but well below the original expectations.

On the seventh day, the Lord may have rested, but not Barth and the wrestling folks who were organizing the United 4 Wrestling event at the Los Angeles Memorial Sports Arena. Sunday was their day to show the world just how well Californians could support the New Vision of international wrestling competition. The event would feature some of the best men and women wrestlers in the world — as well as several notable youth wrestlers from the area.

The organizers caught a break when they learned on Friday that FILA announced a new set of scoring rules for all future international competition. Barth met with the match officials to discuss the possibility of using the new rules on Sunday. Would the officials and wrestlers be sufficiently prepared? They agreed that the Sunday matches would incorporate the new rules, which everyone expected would be a significant improvement over the old, dreaded 'clinch' rules. As it turned out, fans and competitors in attendance applauded the changes and could claim that they were the first ones in history to witness the new FILA rules that afternoon.

Even with all of the last-minute alterations and the mad scramble to try and salvage the event in L.A., the afternoon dual meet brought out the best in international wrestling. The lower two levels of the stands were filled with an enthusiastic crowd roaring from start to finish for the three-plus hours' worth of matches.

In the dual's opening bout, crowd members leapt to their feet and erupted in cheers when Jordan Oliver powered in on a double-leg attack for a takedown late in the match to upend Russia's Magomed Kurbanaliev, 7-6. Oliver, who had just won his second NCAA title for Oklahoma State, later knocked off Olympian and World fifth-place finisher Haislan Garcia of Canada 5-2 in his second bout of the day.

LOS ANGELES... WITHOUT THE IRANIANS

USA's Jordan Oliver won the day's most exciting match with a last-second takedown over his opponent from Russia. Tony Rotundo/WrestlersAreWarriors

"This was incredible," Oliver said of the event. "It's one of the biggest stages in wrestling. It was just an honor to come out and wrestle in such an event. We're all here for a beautiful thing. It's a good cause, and just pushing for that 2020 dream."

The exciting event featured appearances by numerous celebrities and Olympic champions. Mixed Martial Arts stars Randy Couture, Chael Sonnen, Urijah Faber and Daniel Cormier made their appearance. Billy Baldwin was there and helped bring celebrities like his buddy, actor/comedian Tom Arnold, to the Arena. Arnold signed autographs, posed for photos and conducted interviews with the media.

"I'm from Iowa, and Dan Gable is one of my heroes and one of my idols," Arnold told the crowd in Los Angeles. "Wrestling is one of the greatest sports there is and it definitely belongs in the Olympics."

Arnold, who was previously married to actress Roseanne Barr, delivered the funniest line of the day in L.A. after noting that women now wrestle in the Olympics. "I've been married four times," Arnold said, pausing for dramatic effect. "And one of them was to a heavyweight!" The crowd erupted in laughter.

Olympic gold medalists in attendance included Burroughs, Dan Gable, John Smith, Bruce Baumgartner, Henry Cejudo, Tom Brands and Brandon Slay. Past World champion and Super Bowl champion Stephen Neal also spoke to the crowd along with World champions Clarissa Chun, Joe Warren and Adeline Gray.

Patricia Arana, Cade Olivas, Zander Wick and Jaden Abas excited the crowd by winning their youth matches. Besides Oliver, Americans Jon Reader, Chris Pendleton, Elena Pirozhkova, and Brittany Roberts won their international matches leading up to the grand finale — the match everyone was waiting for when Jordan Burroughs stepped on the mat as booming chants of *U-S-A, U-S-A!* echoed off the arena walls.

The powerful, dynamic Burroughs showcased his immense talents in dismantling Russia's Saba Khubetzhty 14-3 in the day's final freestyle match at 74 kg. Burroughs came out firing with his lethal double-leg attacks and finished off the Russian with a series of leg laces as the crowd stood and cheered. He finished the match by technical fall with 32 seconds left in the first period under the new FILA rules.

"I thought it was a lot better here, and the crowd was younger," Burroughs said when comparing the L.A. event to the one in New York. "It was awesome. It was electric. It's cool to be a part of this. California is a very powerful state in wrestling. A lot of great wrestlers come from this area. A lot of important people

LOS ANGELES... WITHOUT THE IRANIANS

Elena Pirozhkova (in blue uniform) was one of two U.S. women to defeat their Canadian opponents at the United 4 Wrestling event in Los Angeles. John Sachs

in wrestling come from this area. It's interesting. It always surprises me when I wrestle around the country to see that there are just as many wrestling fans, and fans of mine, from one place to the next."

By all accounts the United 4 Wrestling event that Sunday afternoon was a major success. Even though the Iranian team did not show, sizable portions of the crowd contained the boisterous Iranian fans, famous for vigorously showing their appreciation for the sportsmen on the mat.

Looking back on that Sunday, Andy Barth remarks, "United 4 Wrestling was successful in ways we hadn't even expected. As the initial event using the new competition rules, we knew from the very first match that wrestling was on the right track and the new rules would make the sport more exciting for viewers. It demonstrated how important women would be to wrestling and how bright the future for women's wrestling is. When those two eight-year-old girls wrestled, it was fabulous. Their attitude, their desire, their skill level, all demonstrated that women's wrestling has tremendous potential. And it showed us the effort that we need to put forward to save our sport. If an eight-year-old can

Even the young (the Olympians of tomorrow, perhaps) wrestlers delighted the L.A. crowd with their wrestling prowess and spirit. John Sachs

love this sport so much that she will fight to the point of exhaustion and actually vomiting after her hand was raised, then that is how hard we all have to fight to keep wrestling in the Olympics."

Dynamic public address announcer Noel Thompson was jubilant, saying: "I was so glad that I went out there and participated in the program. Wrestling took a momentary setback when the Iranians departed early, but we turned it into a marvelous opportunity to again show the world that wrestling is for all nations, all people.

"It was right after the matches that I realized what a huge break we received when the Iranians pulled out and went home," said Thompson. "In Iran, there is no such thing as women's wrestling. Their culture does not allow for it. If Iran's team had stayed and fulfilled their commitment to wrestle in L.A., we would have only scheduled the men's matches; no women's matches. We would likely have been hammered once again by [IOC member Anita] DeFrantz, with the rest of the IOC members listening in."

LOS ANGELES... WITHOUT THE IRANIANS

Instead, DeFrantz wrote in her blog the following day...

Sunday I had the pleasure of attending the United 4 Wrestling event at the Los Angeles Sports Arena. It offered a welcome contrast to last week's Rumble on the Rails in New York, which featured only one women's match out of sixteen. Maybe it was the West Coast, the beautiful sunny day or nothing other than it felt right, but Beat the Streets-Los Angeles and USA Wrestling's presentation of the sport had everything! There were youth wrestlers, boys and girls, as well as national and elite-level wrestlers, men and women. And even though the main guests from Iran chose to go return home after the New York event rather than come to Los Angeles, an enthusiastic crowd was present to see wrestlers from the U.S., Russia and Canada compete under wrestling's new scoring rules. I for one enjoyed the new approach to the ancient sport. Congratulations wrestling. This is the kind of presentation that can help you hold onto your Olympic rings! — Anita.

CHAPTER 17 / **St. Petersburg... Vote #2**

WEDNESDAY, May 29 had been circled on Bill Scherr's calendar for several months — ever since that fateful day in February, actually, when the IOC Executive Board caused a public outcry with their outrageous recommendation to drop wrestling as an Olympic sport. Scherr was now among a handful of senior wrestling administrators and former athletes who were in St. Petersburg, Russia to present their case for keeping wrestling as part of the Games. The IOC invited wrestling, plus seven other sports, to make a presentation to their Executive Board on the afternoon of May 29 for the opportunity to continue their campaign to fill the one vacant slot at the 2020 and 2024 Games — the same spot that opened up when wrestling was given its bad news in February. Directly after the presentations the Executive Board would vote and announce which three of the eight sports would make the shortlist of candidate sports vying for the final vote of approval from the entire IOC General Assembly later in September.

Preparation for St. Petersburg started in March when FILA hired Teneo Strategy to assist its team in preparing the IOC presentation. The parameters were set by the IOC — deliver a 20-minute presentation and allow 10 minutes for questions/answers. The future of Olympic wrestling was at stake — this had to be a crisp, professional presentation that neatly conveyed the key series of messages that FILA wanted the 14 voters on the IOC Executive Board to hear.

CPOW leader Scherr talked about the challenges that wrestling faced in making the shortlist in St. Petersburg: "It is very difficult to overturn the recommendation of the Executive Board that there be 25 core sports, that excludes wrestling, in the September General Assembly meeting in Buenos Aires, Argen-

Daniel Igali, one of 20 siblings and a presenter in St. Petersburg, won his gold medal in wrestling at the 2000 Games in Sydney.

tina. We need to understand that if we don't get placed on the shortlist in May, this whole thing may be over before we begin the fight.

"We are not giving up on the battle that the IOC General Assembly not ratifies the 25 core sport recommendation, but we must acknowledge the difficulty of that process. We must place ourselves in the best possible position to be placed on the shortlist of provisional sports. In May, the Executive Board meets in St. Petersburg at SportAccord, where they lower the number of sports competing for the one provisional sport position from eight to either three or four, to continue to compete against each other at the General Assembly. May is a do-or-die month for us. We need to be named on that shortlist."

One of the first issues that Teneo Strategy addressed with FILA was the makeup of the presentation team. Most items were easy to agree upon: Nenad Lalovic would lead a group of five or six former Olympic athletes; everyone present would have a speaking part; and there had to be diversity, diversity, diversity — which meant presenters hailing from several continents, no more than one American and at least two female team members. Besides the speakers, a professionally designed video would be an integral part of the presentation.

Rich Bender went to work assembling the team. He first reached out to Jim Scherr, the former head of the United States Olympic Committee. He then contacted Daniel Igali, who recently was named head of the Nigerian Wrestling Federation. Igali jumped on board. For the two female spots, Bender called upon Carol Huynh, a 2008 Olympic gold medalist living in Calgary, Canada and Lise Legrand, a 2004 bronze medalist, currently the Vice-President of the French

Wrestling Federation. Originally, Alexander Karelin, the three-time Olympic champion from Siberia, was selected for the team, but he withdrew as a participant due to health issues.

The 32-year-old Huynh talks about her background and her initial reaction to being asked to be a presenter. "My family is originally from China. I was born shortly after my parents moved to Canada in 1980. Ironically, they returned to China to watch me win the Olympics in Beijing in 2008.

"Rich Bender asked me in March to be a presenter in St. Petersburg. At that point, I was kind of like, 'Okay, I can do that.' I almost didn't believe they would want me to play that role. I had a hard time believing they were picking me for such an important role. Terrence Burns from Teneo Strategy worked with me on the speech. I started working with Terrence on my talk about a month-and-a-half before the presentation."

Going into the week, leaders in the wrestling world were cautiously confident that if the presenters made a good showing in front of the IOC, that wrestling would make the shortlist. Their confidence was buoyed when the London book-maker William Hill reported on May 22 that wrestling and squash were in a neck-and-neck race for first place.

"Wrestling has only just been booted out of the Olympics and looks set to make a swift return, although squash, which has been so successful at the Commonwealth Games, will certainly be pushing for inclusion in 2020," remarked William Hill spokesman Joe Crilly.

The full odds from William Hill were as follows...

8:11 Wrestling
7:4 Squash
12:1 Karate
12:1 Wushu
12:1 Sport Climbing
16:1 Baseball/Softball

The presentation team arrived in St Petersburg on Sunday, May 26. Staying in town at the Domina hotel, team members caught up on their sleep and met as a group for the first time on Monday morning. Supporting the team on site was a small contingent of American wrestling leaders — Bender, Dziedzic and Bill Scherr. The consultants led a walk-through of the presentation at the hotel. The group then visited the Convention Center across town where FILA representatives were setting up their booth for the global SportAccord convention where the presentations would take place on Wednesday afternoon.

While the team went through two demanding rehearsals on Tuesday, several decorated wrestling heroes made a grand appearance at the FILA booth at SportAccord. Besides Lalovic, the most prominent were Mikhail Mamiashvili and Saori Yoshida, Japan's recent three-time Olympic champion in women's freestyle. When each appeared for the first time at the booth on Tuesday, a boisterous crowd of press corps reporters and photographers appeared out of nowhere. They surrounded the athletes, hanging onto every word being said and clicking their cameras at will. FILA press chief Bob Condron was all smiles as he was working his plan to have the international media heavily involved with wrestling's quest for redemption.

The presentation team appeared confident and relaxed on Tuesday. They were thankful for the critiques from the consultants — "speak up a bit"; "keep eye contact with members of the IOC"; "don't run over your time limit" were important reminders given to the team.

Igali had relevant experience making similar presentations. He was part of the presentation team for Toronto's 2008 Olympic bid and also a part of Vancouver's 2010 Winter Olympic bid team. He admitted that there was some extra pressure this time around. He pointed out, "In this instance we are trying to regain something that we've had all along; in those other cases we never had it. If wrestling doesn't regain its spot in the Olympics and it was because I screwed up my part of the presentation, well, I don't even want to think about it. Let's just say there's a lot of pressure on all of us."

As the crucial day approached, all the team members expressed confidence in their presentation and their chances of making the shortlist. But no one admitted that they thought wrestling would be a shoo-in. Not even after they read Tuesday's news release from Sportcal, an online daily news service that provides worldwide sports market intelligence....

"The International Olympic Committee's executive board looks set for embarrassment tomorrow when a new ranking of Olympic sports is unveiled, showing that wrestling, the sport recommended by the executive board for exclusion from the 2020 games, is nowhere near the bottom of the rankings.

"It is understood that wrestling ranks somewhere near the middle of the list of the 26 sports that featured on the programme of last year's Olympic Games in London. The sports (and their international federations) have been ranked into groups for the purposes of funding from the IOC.

"The controversial new rankings, which have been decided by a rigorous set of 'objective criteria,' according to Christophe Dubi, the IOC's sports director and deputy Olympic Games executive director, are set to be unveiled at a joint meeting tomorrow morning of the executive boards of the IOC and the Association of

Wrestling's presentation team nervously making last-minute preparations right before going in front of the IOC Executive Board.

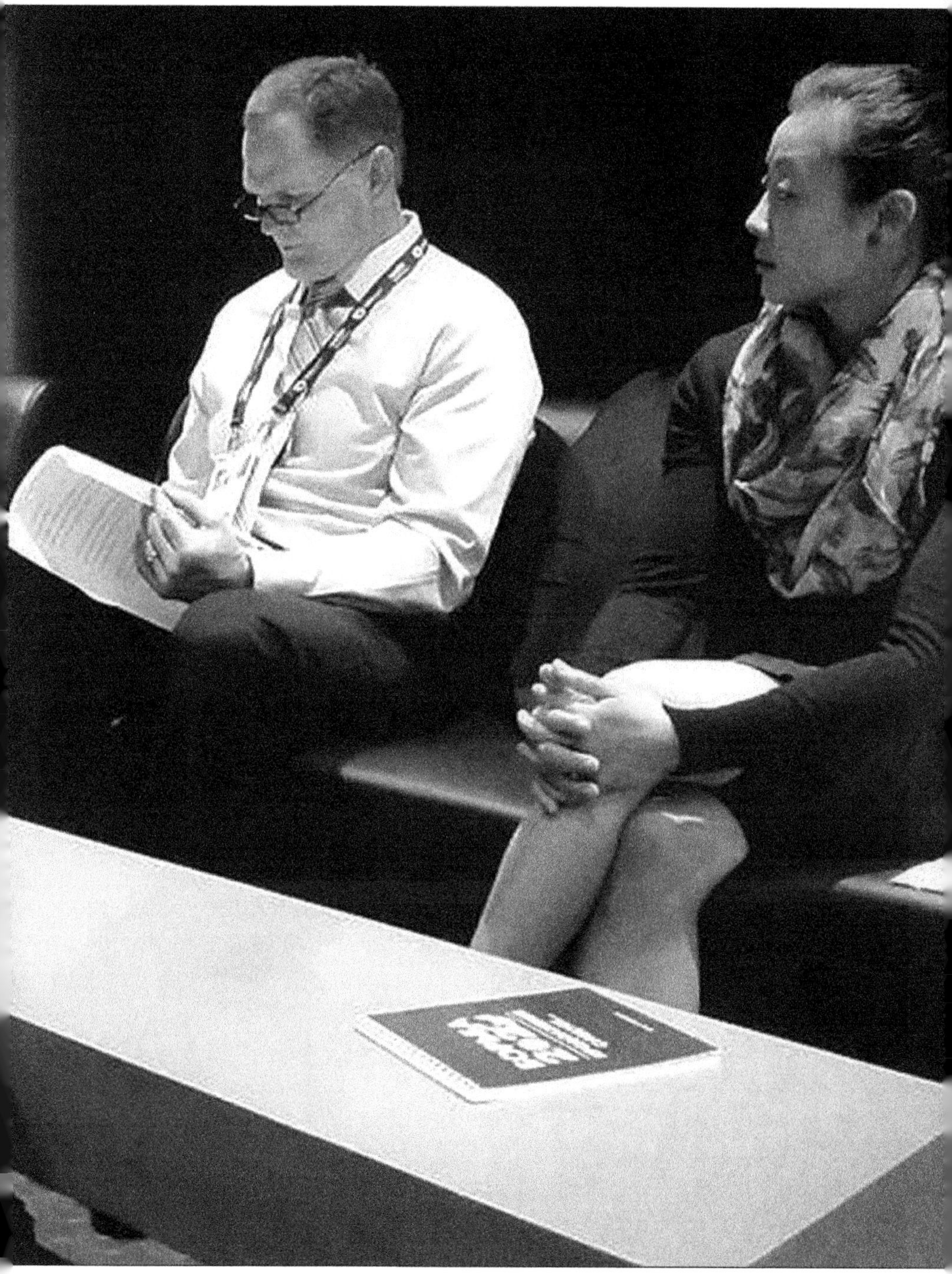

Summer Olympic International Federations at the SportAccord convention in St Petersburg.

"Those criteria are broadly similar — using data from the same London 2012 games — to the criteria that the IOC's programme commission used to present a report on the sports to the IOC's executive board, ahead of its decision in February to recommend wrestling for exclusion from the games.

"It was expected that the report would heavily influence the executive board's recommendation. But not only is wrestling nowhere near the bottom of the funding rankings, it is understood, another sport which survived the recommended cull is close to being isolated at the foot the list."

Yes, it was modern pentathlon, the sport that survived the IOC Executive Board scrutiny back in February, which finished dead last among the 'core' sports in the published rankings.

Of some interest — and concern — on the part of Bender was wrestling's actual ranking as it appeared in the following day's SportAccord newspaper, *The Daily*. While modern pentathlon was alone amongst core Olympic sports in the bottom group (Group E), wrestling was sitting in the next-lowest category (Group D), alongside fencing, handball, and sailing amongst others — yet lower than archery, judo, shooting and weightlifting in Group C. It was reported that the group rankings would have some influence on the level of payments from future Olympics.

The IOC Executive Board went into session early Wednesday afternoon. They allowed five hours in total for the presentations, starting at 2pm local time. The order of presentations was scheduled alphabetically — wrestling would present next to last, at 6pm.

The consultants conducted one last rehearsal early Wednesday afternoon after which the group travelled to the Convention Center to wait their turn to present. Huynh discusses the feeling of the team prior to the presentation: "Were we nervous? Oh yeah, we were all really nervous. Some of us were pacing back and forth, shaking our arms — it was like we were getting ready for a big wrestling match. I would've preferred to just wrestle, that's what I have trained for. That would've been easier for me than giving a speech. We all sounded great in rehearsal. I was confident we would sound fine."

When the group reached the Convention Center at 4pm they were told that the schedule was moving along quickly and that they should be prepared to deliver their presentation around 5pm instead of 6pm. Not a problem for this team —everyone was glad to have the schedule pushed up, not delayed. They were ready.

ST. PETERSBURG... VOTE #2

Shortly after 5pm the presenters were escorted into the conference room to deliver their message to the 15 IOC Executive Board members. Lalovic spoke first. He talked about changes in the constitution and governance and improvements that are being made to better promote the sport.

Lalovic passed it off to Scherr, who talked about rules changes and how they were already making the sport more entertaining and fan-friendly. Scherr was front and center in the presentation. One of the FILA observers in St. Petersburg remarked, "Jim's insights and instincts were important in developing and executing what needed to be done to save wrestling. His role in the presentations was that of a professional Olympic administrator and he filled the role well."

Scherr introduced Legrand, who spoke about the Women's Commission and suggestions they will be proposing to FILA to support women, such as annual coaches and officials clinics designed for women.

Igali was next. His talk was short but heart-felt...

Good afternoon everyone, I'm Daniel Igali, Sydney gold medalist. The saying goes, 'To wrestle is to be human.' As one of 20 siblings growing up in a poor village in my native Nigeria, I can tell you that if I had not learned how to wrestle well, I may not have gotten very much to eat. So, in a very real way, wrestling taught me how to survive.

By age 20, I was the African National Wrestling Champion but I realized that Nigeria did not have the resources to help me continue my Olympic dream. Due to the political instability in my country, I made the decision to apply for Canadian citizenship, where I continued my wrestling and academic education. At the Sydney Games in 2000, I was fortunate to win the gold medal — Canada's first, and, in a very personal but unofficial way — Nigeria's first. I am here to tell you that I am very proud of both of those facts.

I moved back to Nigeria to help young children — athletes or not. I wanted to create an environment where youngsters did not have to leave home to pursue their dreams, or even to have a dream. I am an example of how the sport of wrestling changed one life — mine — and how it can change the lives of other young people in my home country. To wrestle is indeed to be human, but often the competition is not on the mat, it is often in the heart and in the mind.

I want to see wrestling remain on the Olympic program to help inspire the next little boy or little girl wrestling for the resources not only to live, but also to succeed. Thank you.

Then Igali turned it over to Huynh for the group's final words to the IOC. Like Igali, Huynh spoke from the heart, perhaps with even more emotion...

Good afternoon. I'm Carol Huynh. I am an Olympian. I'm a Chinese-Cana-

dian and I'm a woman. But most of all, I am a wrestler.

My parents are originally from China, but they've been refugees twice: first to Vietnam in the 50s and then to Canada in 1980. Needless to say, my parents are determined and hard-working people. Their simple goal was to create a better life for their family. I don't think they ever imagined that their example would lead their daughter back to China for an Olympic gold medal, or to London for a bronze. Olympism seems to work in mysterious ways.

My family's work ethic was perfect for wrestling. As a kid I played just about every sport I could and then I found wrestling. I fell in love with it. Its combative nature cultivated the determination and fighting spirit that you need in the pursuit of excellence.

As a woman, wrestling has given me strength and confidence and it empowered me to my full potential. It takes courage to step out on the mat with that tight singlet on, with no armor and no equipment other than your hands, your heart, and your mind. The Olympics gave me a dream to pursue. I wonder what will happen to those young girls who might not get a chance to follow a similar dream?

Being an Olympian made me a part of history, a role model for young people and I want future generations of young female — and male — wrestlers to believe that they can make history too.

Thank you all for your work in making Olympic dreams real for women like me.

The presentation was greatly enhanced by the playing of two videos for the IOC Board. The first video opened with numerous young boys and girls from all over the world saying, "I want to be an Olympian," followed up with short clips of these young wrestlers in competition, including a still of the eight-year-old girl in Los Angeles strutting onto the mat. According to the team, the best part was the video that played at the closing of the presentation. The film focused in on the faces of these boys and girls as the lyric of the music played: "Look into my eyes."

A FILA official who had seen the video remarked, "If we don't succeed, it will be those eyes that will haunt me."

As the presentation concluded, the team noted that through their body language, the IOC members seemed to approve of the presentation. In fact, one of them even started clapping.

Huynh recalls the hours between the presentation and the IOC announcement of the three sports making the shortlist. "When we came out after the presentation, it was crazy. There was a huge crowd of media folks surrounding Mr. Lalovic and the rest of the group. We were kind of part of the entourage. They

ST. PETERSBURG... VOTE #2   117

Head of the Japan Wrestling Federation, Tomiaki Fukuda, with Saori Yoshida and Nenad Lalovic at the FILA booth during the SportAccord Convention.

were all there before we went up the escalator to make the presentation and they were all there when we came down afterwards. People were clapping and cheering when we came down the escalator after the presentation. It was really cool. We knew none of the other sports had that kind of attention.

"The waiting after the presentation was the hardest part. After we finished our speech we waited about two hours, which seemed like a really long time."

The IOC press conference was scheduled for 8:30pm. Around 7pm the IOC announced that they had completed their voting and were moving the announcement up one hour. No one complained about this change to the schedule.

As 7:30 approached, the large ballroom began to fill. The press occupied the first several rows. In the front row of the spectator section sat the wrestling contingent — the five presenters plus others from FILA, USA Wrestling, and the Russian Federation. Bender recalls, "Just before the official announcement was made, Lalovic came up and motioned me to walk toward him. He leaned in and whispered in my ear, 'We're through.' Someone from the IOC had informed him we were in."

Three IOC representatives took the podium — IOC Communications Director Mark Adams, Program Commission Chair Franco Carraro and Sports Director Chris Dubi. After some brief introductory remarks, Adams announced the verdicts.

A large surge of cheer erupted from the wrestling contingent and the press corps when wrestling was the first sport announced as one of the three moving forward. Huynh remembers the moment: "When we heard the decision, it was just a huge sigh of relief. My eyes were tearing up a little bit. It was really emotional when we were heard the decision."

Moments after the announcement that wrestling had made the shortlist, the IOC staff leaders informed the crowd that baseball/softball and squash would be the other two sports on the ballot when the 103-person General Assembly votes in Buenos Aires in September.

There was significance in the fact that wrestling was the first sport voted in. Shortly after the announcement it was revealed that wrestling won the majority vote on the first ballot – eight YES votes to six votes in total for an assortment of other sports. The votes in the next rounds for the other two sports were not so clear-cut...

Round 2

1st ballot: karate 5, wushu 4, squash 2, baseball/softball 1, climbing 1... roller and wake eliminated.

2nd ballot: karate and wushu 4, baseball/softball 3, squash 2, climbing 1... climbing eliminated.

3rd ballot: karate and wushu 4, baseball/softball 3, squash 3... go to run-off. Run-off: baseball/softball 8, squash 6... squash eliminated.

4th ballot: baseball/softball 6, karate and wushu 4... go to run-off. Run-off: karate 9, wushu 5... wushu eliminated.

5th ballot: baseball/softball 9, karate 5
Baseball/softball is short-listed

Round 3

1st ballot: karate 5, wushu 4, squash 3, climbing 2

2nd ballot: squash 5, wushu 4, climbing 3, karate 2... karate eliminated

3rd ballot: squash 8, wushu 4, climbing 2... squash is short-listed

Only the IOC could dream up such a voting system! Karate and wushu received a total of nine votes on the first ballot of round two and round three but neither survived the final cut. Look at the baseball/softball vote pattern in round two. One doesn't have to wonder for long if certain deals were made.

Meanwhile, the immediate thought on the minds of those in the wrestling party was, "Now what, what do we need to do for Argentina?"

Dziedzic commented, "Well, it's like we just won the semi-finals bout. We are happy, but we still have to go out and win in the finals in Buenos Aires."

Chapter 18 / **Enter Phase Two**

THE IOC VOTE In St. Petersburg essentially ended Phase One of the Save Olympic Wrestling campaign and signaled the start of Phase Two. Gary Abbott describes the difference in the overall approach: "The first phase was very active, lots of activities, lots of public events, lots of PR. It was wrestling against seven foes. It was intense. Phase Two was much more subtle, but was marked with two big items — the event in ancient Olympia and the move to the 6-6-6 weight classes for the 2016 Games. In this phase, wrestling was the leader, the favorite — we had to make sure we kept on a path towards victory.

"The recurring theme of Phase One was to have something going on all the time and publicize the hell out of it. Big events — big drumbeat!" says Abbott, who singled out Roger Frizzell for his contribution during this most critical time.

"Public relations was the biggest part of the CPOW budget and a major focus of the FILA effort," said Abbott. "Why was it that the message about the positive changes taking place in wrestling was heard by the IOC and the world? This was not an accident. It may have been the biggest success of the entire activity. The glue behind the PR effort in Phase One was Roger Frizzell, without a doubt one of the big heroes of this entire endeavor.

"Roger took the time to bring together the right team of PR professionals and made sure they worked together well, right from day one. Roger was able to get USA Wrestling staff, its PR firm Ketchum, its marketing firm KOM, and the individual members of CPOW and others to effectively work as a team. The volume of work coming out of this area was massive and necessary in Phase One."

Abbott concludes, "John Bardis called Frizzell 'the best PR professional he had ever worked with.' That assessment is accurate."

Frizzell had to step down from his public relations leadership role in Phase Two due to a change in his career (he moved to Florida to take over the PR responsibilities for Carnival Cruise Lines), yet he continued to provide advice on a timely basis to the CPOW team.

After the favorable IOC vote in St. Petersburg, Rich Bender offered his views on Phase Two: "Moving forward, we can't take the approach that we are a front runner going into this September 8 vote. Nobody really knows that. I've been around enough private IOC voting processes to know that anything can happen in a situation like this. We don't know what those 103 people in the IOC are thinking. Nobody really does.

"As Jim Scherr once said, 'The [IOC] issue is not decided until the bar is closed the night before the vote.'

According to insiders, Roger Frizzell's PR acumen was one of the biggest contributors to the success of wrestling's campaign to save the Olympic sport.

"I'm very optimistic about our chances in September, but we've got a tremendous amount of work left to do before then. We've built some momentum and we've done some positive things, but we obviously have to keep this going right until that vote."

Bender and others were also trying to sort out what precisely would be the procedure for selecting the winning sport in Buenos Aires. The IOC Executive Board had set the parameters — 25 'core' sports, plus three 'provisional' sports would be on the 2020 and 2024 Olympic program. Two of the 'provisional' sports were already chosen by the IOC in 2009 — golf and rugby sevens. The third 'provisional' sport (making 28 sports in total) would be selected from the St. Petersburg shortlist.

Word filtered down that two separate votes would take place in Buenos Aires at the IOC General Assembly meeting. The first vote would be to ratify the IOC recommendation of February 12 that wrestling no longer be included as one of the 25 'core' Olympic sports.

If that vote was *not* ratified, wrestling would likely remain as a 'core' sport and the IOC would be sailing in unchartered waters. At the time, no one seemed to know exactly what would happen next if the February recommendation was not ratified. Perhaps another Executive Board vote on dropping a different sport? Perhaps not eliminating any sport — nor adding any sport? Perhaps keeping wrestling and voting between baseball/softball and squash as the 27th sport (making 29 sports in total)?

If the General Assembly did ratify the February 12 recommendation, as many expected, then wrestling, baseball/softball and squash would give their presentations and immediately face a secret-ballot vote for the one open spot. The sport that received the majority of the General Assembly votes in this second election on September 8 would be added as a 'provisional' sport for the 2020 and 2024 Games. If wrestling was successful, FILA would then have to demonstrate over that period of time that wrestling should be permanently returned to the Olympics as a 'core' sport.

FILA's Dziedzic talks a little about the organization's strategy leading up to those two votes in September: "As I've stated before, wrestling must remain on the sideline regarding the first vote concerning the ratifying of the IOC recommendation or risk alienating the very people it needs to be reinstated. Wrestling must be seen as vying for one of the three remaining slots, not overturning the IOC Executive Board's previous recommendation. A recent note to the FILA Bureau from Martinetti advises otherwise, but everyone else is in line with this thinking.

"The Association of National Olympic Committees [ANOC] President Sheikh Al-Sabah has been a supporter of wrestling from the get-go. In its last meeting shortly after the IOC vote, which Nenad Lalovic attended by the way, ANOC declared its support for wrestling. If the IOC General Assembly doesn't ratify the Executive Board's recommendation, it will be someone from this group that most likely leads the charge."

In a *Washington Post* column Tracee Hamilton remarked on wrestling's fall: "The real shame is that it took a near-death blow by the IOC to get the attention of the sport. Being reinstated as a provisional sport is a long step down from being a 'core' sport. But it is wrestling's best — and perhaps last — chance. Here's hoping the sport makes it through the repechage and back into the main draw where it belongs."

In an attempt to get back into that main draw, FILA began working with TSE Consulting in developing a worldwide strategic plan for wrestling. In early June the President of the Qatar Wrestling Federation (QWF) Zamel Sayyaf Al Shahrani talked about this move in an interview with Mohamed Al Malki, AIPS Vice-President: "Currently, we are working with the TSE Consulting group. The group is working all over the world to get feedback from the spectators, wrestlers, referees and everybody who matters. The first such exercise began in Qatar. The TSE officials will be visiting

ENTER PHASE TWO 123

Martinetti Raphaël
FILA Bureau member
1920 Martigny

        Mr. Nenad Lalovic
        FILA President
        Rue du Château 6
        1804 Corsier-sur-Vevey

Martigny, 10 July 2013

Subject: Strategy for Buenos Aires

Dear Mr. President,

With no surprise, wrestling was retained by IOC's Executive Board as part of the three sports that will be put forward in Buenos Aires to enter the 2020-2024 Olympic programme. That first step was pure justice since the EB would have violated the Olympic Charter if it had not retained wrestling at Saint-Petersburg's presentation, but I however congratulate you for that first victory.

The real battle is therefore only starting, since the final decision falls to the IOC Session next September. We must do our utmost to repair the injustice that the EB inflicted to our sport by making sure the IOC Session rejects EB's proposal to withdraw wrestling from the list of core sports.

That strategy requires an active participation from all Bureau members and National Federations concerned on the basis of personal contacts with the IOC members who have the power to reject EB's shameful proposal.

I therefore ask you to gather the FILA Bureau – or if you prefer the Executive Committee – and divide up the IOC members among the Bureau members and National Federations and assign them with the mission to plead our case to the IOC members who are expecting contact from us.

The two other sports that are fighting to enter the Olympic programme have already started to lobby and we head for disaster if we do not take action immediately.

I hope you will implement that strategy and soon share out the missions between the Bureau members and National Federations concerned.

        Sincerely yours,

        Raphaël Martinetti
        FILA Bureau member

Cc: FILA Bureau members

Raphy Martinetti's letter advising FILA on its strategy going into the Buenos Aires IOC vote — his suggestions were ignored by the organization.

The wrestling matches between the USA, Canada and Ukraine in Niagara Falls gained world-wide attention for greater gender equity for women's wrestling. Larry Slater

different countries to get feedback and accordingly a plan will be devised.

"FILA leadership believes that putting a strategic plan in place will ensure that a common framework is created within which the sport, represented by the national governing bodies around the world, can work together towards common goals for the future."

In addition, FILA moved to the second phase of its advertising campaign, with a new slogan... 'All Nations. All People. For All Time.' This reflected some of the themes that are central to the sport: wrestling is everywhere, wrestling is for everyone and wrestling is an original Olympic sport.

Back on the wrestling mats, a strategic event was taking place in Canada just two days after the St. Petersburg conclave. The brainchild of USA Wrestling's Abbott, Battle at the Falls took over the headlines at the resort city of Niagara Falls. The event featured a women's freestyle wrestling tournament involving teams from the United States, Canada and the Ukraine. The dual on Friday, May 31 capped World Wrestling Month and received worldwide publicity for women's wrestling.

The USA team defeated Ukraine 16-13 but fell to the champions from Canada,

Among the celebrities at the Battle at the Falls was Dan Gable, who voiced his support for the growth of women's wrestling. Larry Slater

18-10. Veronica Carlson won her bout against Canada's Stacie Anaka in a battle of past Junior World medalists at 67 kg/147.5 lbs. She was not unaware of the significance and timing of the tournament. "This event was really important," Carlson said. "A big factor with the International Olympic Committee is gender equality. Women's wrestling is a growing sport. To capitalize on this event here is so important for us as a global community of women's wrestlers."

Tamara Medwidsky, Executive Director of Wrestling Canada, commented in an internet blog: "USA Wrestling has been amazing partners in this event. The event was a great opportunity for women wrestling and showcased the new rules that FILA adopted in the recent weeks. Marty Calder and his club [Brock Wrestling Club] have stepped up to the plate, and once again delivered a world-class event."

Dan Gable was one of the wrestling dignitaries attending Battle of the Falls. Gable's background is with men's folkstyle and freestyle wrestling, but he's also followed the women's freestyle program closely in recent years.

"The morning I was heading up to Niagara Falls, my flight got delayed and then it got delayed again, but I made it up there," he said. "I needed to be there for that

Athletes and coaches from all three women's teams enjoyed the gorgeous view of the Falls during their stay in Canada.

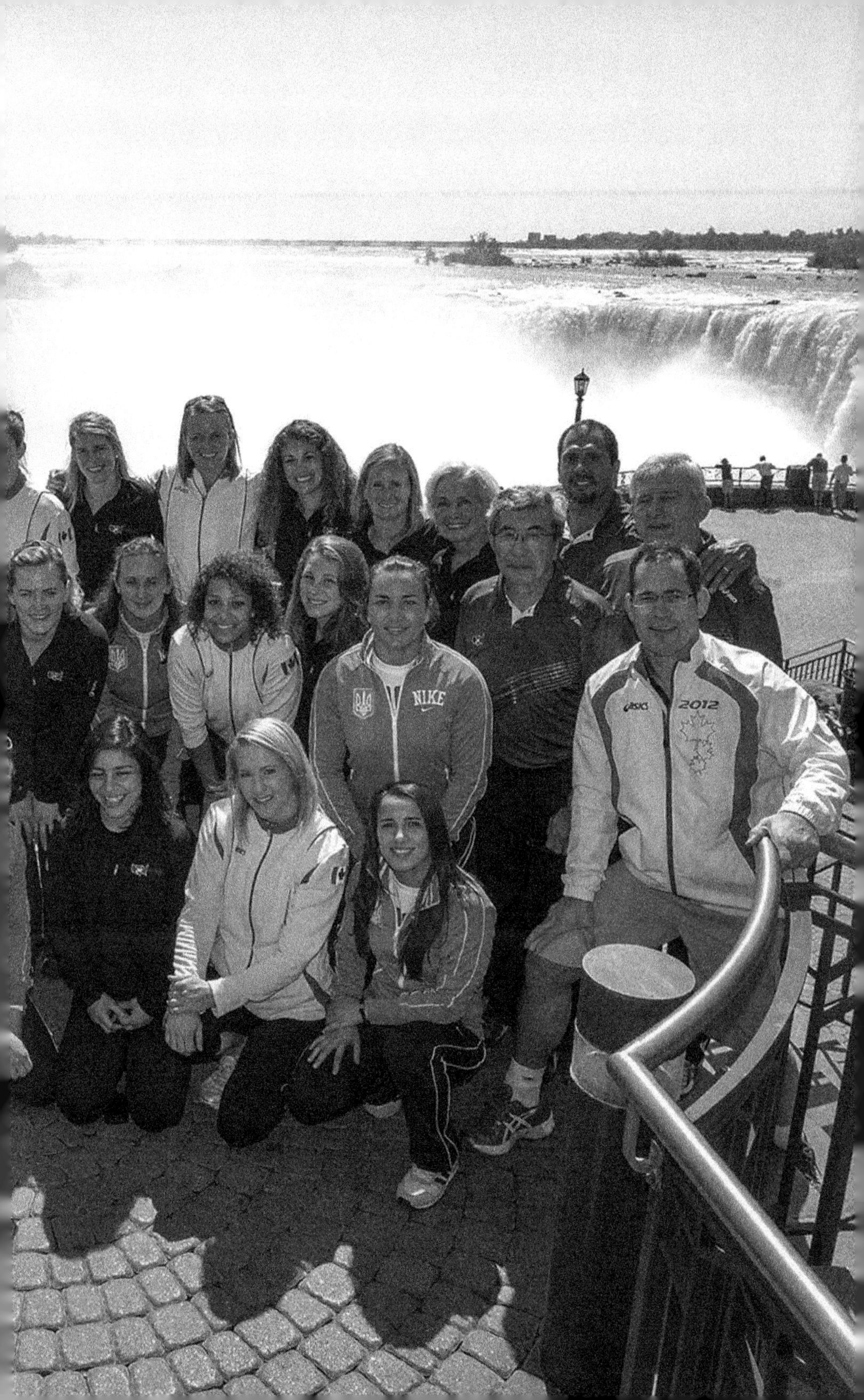

NIKE
ASICS
2012

event — I felt like it was really important that I be there to support women's wrestling. Gender equity is a big issue that the IOC had with international wrestling. I was hoping to draw a little more attention to women's wrestling, and I probably did seven or eight interviews in Niagara Falls.

"I'm very impressed with the quality and the caliber of women's wrestling — they have really improved. The girls have developed and progressed just like the guys have. It helps to have full-time coaches like Terry Steiner working with the women. We need to keep doing more with the women to keep wrestling in the Olympics."

Gable was surprised that so many young Canadian boys and girls wrestlers approached him for autographs at the Niagara Falls event. "It's amazing that these kids even knew who I was — that fires me up to know maybe I can inspire some of them," Gable said. "They may not be Olympic caliber right now, but in their mind that is what they are shooting for. And some of them might end up being Olympians some day. We need to keep the Olympic dream alive for kids like that."

Comments from IOC leadership after the St. Petersburg presentation led most observers to believe that FILA was finally addressing the gender equality problems that existed in the sport for decades. Coming out of that IOC session were signs that there would likely be an increase in the number of weight classes for women wrestlers in the 2016 Olympics, and the FILA Bureau would add one woman vice-president to the international decision-making group in the near future.

President Jacques Rogge was quoted as saying, "If you look at the reaction of the federation to their admitted shortcomings, the international federation drastically changed its own governance, including [installing] women in the executive board — which was a criticism of the report from the IOC — changing the format of the competition, changing the presentation."

Gender equity was just one of the issues on the table as wrestling leaders in the United States defined their plans to win the deciding vote in Buenos Aires.

Many of the CPOW members, consultants and other key leaders in the wrestling community in the U.S. met on Monday, June 17 in Chicago. The purpose of the meeting was to lay out their plans and strategy over the next 12 weeks, leading up to the IOC general assembly vote.

The predominant theme coming out of the meeting was CPOW's determination to provide strong, timely assistance to FILA in their thrust to win the IOC vote in September. In particular, the group focused on helping with...

• Increasing public relations and communications support. CPOW proposed to develop a public relations plan and link it with FILA's plan, with the assistance of USA Wrestling staff and consulting resources from KOM, Ketchum and Teneo.

• Organizing a wrestling exhibition in Greece near an ancient Olympic site.

- Continuing to personally meet or communicate with IOC members to ensure that all General Assembly voters are aware of the changes that wrestling is making.
- Driving social media, such as Facebook and Twitter, traffic to FILA.
- Exploring the potential for expanding the Beat the Streets concept overseas, dovetailing it with the development centers FILA has already set up.
- Working with event specialists outside of wrestling to review sport presentation.
- Providing assistance as needed for the Buenos Aires presentation.
- Providing supplementary funding for special FILA events and projects.

CPOW leader Bill Scherr concluded the meeting by reaffirming the group's sense of urgency and support of FILA. He also directed some counsel to the international organization, such as...

- Demonstrate progress on the promised changes – new rules implemented, gender equity issues addressed, athletes and women added to the Bureau, etc.
- Publicize the consultant's (TSE) plans and strategy in the development of a 'Strategic Plan for Wrestling' before the Buenos Aires presentation.
- Expand the PR message beyond 'change'; it should also emphasize the positive characteristics of wrestling (global, accessible, and inexpensive) that make it a perfect fit for the Olympics.

One week later consultant Andrew Craig met with the CPOW group in Chicago. Word coming out of the meeting was that Craig presented three key points that were well received by the attendees...

1. We need to be very specific in our approach to get at least 53 votes. Anything not on that path is wasted energy.

2. FILA, the consultants and groups like CPOW need to communicate and coordinate the messaging and plans.

3. There is not much time. We simply do not have the luxury of time. We must move quickly and we can't afford mistakes.

Chapter 19 / **6-6-6**

OTHER THAN the change to the 'new rules' of wrestling, probably the most controversial issue that FILA and the national federations had to deal with post-February IOC recommendation was the number of weight classes to be contested at future Olympic Games. There were numerous complicating factors to consider. Such as...

• Since 2004, the weight classes contested have been: seven for men's freestyle; seven for men's Greco-Roman: four for women's freestyle. Should FILA propose the same number of weight classes (18) contested in total for men and women as there had been for the last three Olympics? Or more? Or less?

• IOC President Rogge had set a limit on the number of Games participants (believed to be 10,500 in total). It was generally agreed at a meeting between IOC representatives and FILA back in March that it would be unwise for wrestling to propose to the IOC that it was adding weight classes and participants while trying to win their vote to stay part of the Games.

• With the goal of greater gender equality, should the women have as many weight classes contested as the men? In total? Or just in freestyle?

• If additional weight classes were added for the women, what would the reaction be if there was an offsetting reduction in the men's weight classes — the 6-6-6 scenario?

• Should an alternative equity solution be implemented, such as having an equal number of male and female freestylers participating in the Games in a 7-7-7 or 8-8-8 format, with a reduced number of qualifiers (entries)?

• Should the Greco-Roman discipline be eliminated, as some had proposed, so that freestyle could have eight or nine weight classes each for men and women?

- Should changes be made immediately (that is, starting with the 2016 Games in Rio de Janeiro) or wait until 2020 if/when wrestling was voted back into the Games?
- Would announcing a change — one that includes greater participation by female wrestlers in 2016 — prior to the IOC General Assembly vote in September have a significant positive influence on those IOC voters?

After much discussion, FILA President Lalovic and his close confidantes believed that the most fair and favorable number of weight classes to be contested in the 2016 Olympics was...

Six for men's freestyle;
Six for men's Greco-Roman;
Six for women's freestyle.

President Lalovic sought and received a mail-in vote of FILA Bureau members regarding their preference for implementing the weight class configuration change for the 2016 Olympic Games.

Several Bureau members wrote letters voicing the opinion that these changes should NOT be implemented in 2016. Two such letters follow, the first from former Hungarian Olympic wrestling champion Dr. Csaba Hegedüs...

Dear Mr. President!

I wish to thank you for your email message in which you were asking for the opinion of the FILA Bureau regarding the participation of wrestling at the 2016 Olympic Games in Rio de Janeiro and the composition of the Referees' Commission.

First of all I wish to emphasize my disagreement that fundamental issues like the ones here strongly influencing the future of our sport be decided through postal vote of simple yes or no with 3-4 days allowed for thinking.

My opinion concerning the two questions is as follows.

Rio de Janeiro 2016, 6-6-6

I believe that first we should ask for the opinion of NFs, the athletes, coaches just as it happened in connection with the recent modification of the rules. The proposal is talking about six categories per style. Which are they? Do you already have a proposal for that as well? Are we pushed by time factor or under pressure to make such a hasted decision?

I did not happen to find any implication of this situation in Mr. Dubi's email message of June 7 as he was inquiring if "some of the measures proposed for 2020 will already apply for the Rio Olympic Games." Or are there any further infomation that I might not be aware of?

In full agreement with Mr. Fukuda's proposal in his earlier letter. I believe that these and many more issues should be discussed and decided at an official Bureau meeting as soon as possible.

Although before London we were talking about the expansion of the women's sector now the proposal of a total change of categories (at men actually a cut of two) is lying ahead of us which is a very serious question between two Olympic Games. I think that this change will find most of the countries unprepared. Multitude of countries do not have broad base to rely on with more than one athlete of same value in one category. They are compelled to build their wrestlers individually by mobilizing huge amounts of financial, material and human resources through the years. For them one single bronze medal can be an enormous achievement securing the survival of wrestling in these nations. I am convinced that this change will have negative effect at most of them.

I think that in Buenos Aires not this issue (6-6-6) will be the secret of success. After St. Petersburg we had every reason to be happy and proud to say that wrestling was able to show its strength by qualifying as sole sport in the first round. One of FILA's main tasks is to fight for wrestling's widest universal representation and serve its best interests internationally where of course the Olympic Games play a leading role and where we have been successful so far. I think that wrestling must have the necessary power and strength to battle for further positions and we should not let existing ones go. Positions lost by self- made decisions are very hard if not impossible to get back. Ever.

Dear Mr. President!

Were you thinking about the alternative of determining the equity of genders on a higher level (7-7-7 instead of 6-6-6) and start lobbying at IOC for this goal?

A proper starting point for this can be provided by the fact that a new president will be elected by the IOC Session in Buenos Aires. As I could go through the opinions, visions of the future of the candidates published in the international media, I could realize that several of them are not contrary to the idea of Olympic expansion since the 302 Olympic disciplines and the maximum of 10500 athletes was the limit continuously uttered and supported by Mr. Rogge.

Your clarification regarding the second bronze medal would also be most appreciated as your letter was not clear about this very important issue. You write that with the proposed new formula "we keep the same number of wrestlers and medals than in London 2012" while in the next sentence you say "we will be in a much better position to... renegotiate the number of bronze medals."

According to my information an IOC meeting shall take place in Lausanne on July 3-4 where the presidential candidates shall submit their programmes and ideas. I believe that this could be an excellent opportunity for FILA to keep on its lobby and collect valuable information that might help our mission for Buenos Aires.

I do not support the idea of the proposal and the 6-6-6 categories either as I do not consider them timely and relevant.
With friendly regards
Dr. Csaba Hegedüs

Naturally, the increasingly out-of-touch Martinetti was also keen to offer his opinions...

Subject: Proposals Rio 2016
Mister President,
I acknowledge receipt, with pleasure, of your circular letter of 16 June in which you ask — for once — the Bureau's opinion before making a decision that will affect the future of wrestling.
I answered negatively to both your proposals and the purpose of this letter is to explain why:
A) To propose IOC 6 categories of GR, FS and FW for Rio 2016
That proposal will have no influence whatsoever on IOC's decision to reinstate wrestling as part of the core sports in Buenos Aires. Wrestling is on the program of the Rio Olympics and that change will only give additional arguments to those who wanted to eliminate wrestling in order to save their own sport.
Jacques Rogge had already made that proposal for the London Olympics and the Bureau rejected it.
The modification of the number of weight categories for Rio 2016 requires an extensive consultation with the National Federations to assess:

- *Which category to cancel*
- *Which categories to modify*
- *Which countries and continents would be penalised by the removal of one category*

That proposal will by no means soften certain IOC members' dislike of Greco-Roman since they have long requested to keep only one wrestling style.
Here are, Mr. President, the reasons that made me refuse your proposals.
It is however obvious that once wrestling will be reinstated as part of the 2020-2024 Olympic program, we will be able to negotiate the program, styles and categories with IOC, without flattening ourselves.
Yours sincerely,
Raphaël Martinetti
FILA Bureau member
cc: FILA

In a letter of June 25 to the FILA Bureau members, President Lalovic announced the results of the mail-in vote...

18 members voted in favor of implementing the 6-6-6 format in 2016; 7 voted against.

This decision was not formally announced by FILA until August.

Raphy Martinetti wrote Lalovic asking for a head count ("who voted for what") of the votes. His request was denied.

As a side note to the 6-6-6 vote, on the same ballot sent to all Bureau members in June was the question of whether Ik-Jong Kim should remain as head of the FILA Referee Commission. This was a much more private, yet still controversial, issue for FILA to address. Kim had been re-confirmed at the Phuket Bureau meeting in February, primarily because he was the sole referee on the FILA Bureau.

Back in the spring, the IOC's Chris Dubi suggested that FILA's Referee Commission needed more independence and that the group's governance would improve if the Commission were not headed by a Bureau member. Lalovic responded by appointing Finland's Karri Toivola to replace Kim. Kim objected and threatened to take the issue to CAS. Lalovic responded that the announcement was premature and then asked for the Bureau vote (along with the 6-6-6 vote). The Bureau supported Lalovic's decision by a 3-1 margin. Despite the vote against him, Kim has appealed to CAS for a hearing on the matter.

Just another bump in the road on the way to Buenos Aires...

Meanwhile back on the weight-class configuration issue, the vote for the 6-6-6 format seemed to overcome one of wrestling's biggest issues regarding the women. In all the non-Olympic years, the women competed in the World Championships and other FILA events in seven weight classes, same as the men. But since the Olympics only recognized just four female weights, many women had to compete at either a higher or lower weight class for that Olympic-year cycle. Now with six weights available for competition, the strain on the 'tweeners' should not be as grueling.

A couple of America's most outstanding women's wrestlers were pleased with the outcome. Colorado native Adeline Gray, 2012 world champion at 67kg, talked about the addition of two women's Olympic weight classes starting in 2016. "Going to 6-6-6 is exciting. Having those two extra spots at the Olympics will make a big difference. It was always difficult trying to squeeze women wrestlers into just four weight classes. It was very difficult to wrestle at your optimum weight. Many girls were caught between weight classes when going for the Olympics."

Gray was unhappy, though, about the loss of men's weights. She continues, "I am very disappointed that they have to take weight classes away from the men. I

USA's Adeline Gray, a World champion, likes the increase from four to six women's weight classes but not at the expense of the men.

wish everyone had eight weights.

"It's a difficult subject to deal with. Like Title IX, the problem is how it is implemented. They should not have to subtract from the men. Women are just trying to compete — we don't want to take away from the men. But I'm a bit afraid men will look at the results and say 'women took away our spots.'

"Women's wrestling is really growing and I agree with those that say women can be the ones to save the sport of wrestling. Women's wrestling is the largest growth area of the sport. I love the fact that we now have a female, Seiko Yamamoto, on our USA women's freestyle coaching staff.

"We need to change the stigma that the worst thing in life for a guy is losing to a girl. That ripples through life on and off the mat. That good ole boy culture is not a good culture.

"Personally, I've been fortunate to have received such great support all along in my wrestling career. The guys in high school really respected me as an athlete. Many saw the bigger picture — we were all competing in a sport we loved."

Helen Maroulis, ranked second in the world by FILA at 55kg, has been wrestling since she was seven years old and remembers all her Olympic dreams. "I don't ever remember not having the dream of being an Olympic champion. When I started out, women's wrestling wasn't an Olympic sport. Mom said maybe I shouldn't do this because there is no future. But at the Sydney Olympics, they announced that women's wrestling would be an Olympic sport starting in 2004. When she heard that news mom said, 'Well, maybe there is a future for you in the sport.'"

She continues, "It's a tough spot. Naturally I want more weight classes for women. We have such a growing sport. But I hate to hear that they might be taking weight classes and medal opportunities away from the men in order to do this. I don't want that. Plus, I hear rumors that they might drop Greco-Roman wrestling. I have some great friends that wrestle Greco and I don't want to see it eliminated."

Kyle Dake is delighted to see the progress that women are making in wrestling. "Women's wrestling is on the rise. I think it is important to give them the chance to compete in more than just four weight classes. It will allow for a lot more talent in the Olympic competition," said Dake.

"Anyone can be a wrestler," continued Dake. "You don't have to be a male; it's not like football. I think it's really, really cool to have the women wrestle. I wish they'd add more weight classes so each discipline could have eight to 10 weights. We'd then have a lot more very good wrestlers involved."

Long-time men and women's wrestling coach Ron Tirpak sums up the general feelings: "No doubt the current proposal will antagonize the men. They feel that they've already given up something, dropping from 10 weight classes to seven when women's Olympic wrestling came aboard. Now they probably have to lose another weight class. It's difficult for them to understand. But for the women, the change will give us equality — having six weight classes is tremendously better than just four."

Dziedzic defends the notion of keeping Greco as an Olympic discipline — at least for now. He points out that FILA has a vested interest in maximizing the number of weight classes in both the World Championships and the Olympics. Wrestling's relative importance in the Olympic program is directly related to the number of weight classes contested and disciplines. He concludes, "Sacrificing Greco-Roman to establish gender equity and maintaining seven weight classes per discipline would most likely have disintegrated wrestling's united front. Gone would be Sweden, Finland, Norway, Poland, Kazakhstan, Denmark and Hungary; Russia's enthusiasm and support would've been diminished."

Lee Roy Smith and Dan Gable take a rational approach in their view of the reconstructed weight categories. Smith, Executive Director of the National Wrestling Hall of Fame says, "I am not so sure FILA has to live with the 6-6-6 weight categories forever. These recommendations were driven by the importance that the IOC places on gender equality. There are rational arguments to this proposal that may be better challenged after we get back in the Games. I hope so, because I don't like the fact that wrestling is now below the number of weights they have for boxing and judo."

Gable puts it succinctly regarding the present restructuring of the Olympic weight classes to a 6-6-6 format: "If that's the best solution for now, I would take that over having no wrestling at all in the Olympics," he said. "You get wrestling back in the Olympics and when it's more stable then you prove that we need 8-8-8. You hate to take away any weight classes, but that may be the reality for now. It's a lot better than 0-0-0."

CHAPTER 20 / **The New Rules**

OF ALL THE changes that FILA made to the sport of wrestling following the IOC recommendation to eliminate it from the Olympics, none made more of an immediate impact on the wrestling community than the 'new rules'.

No other change was embraced as much as the 'new rules'.
No other change was debated as much as the 'new rules'.
No other change was tinkered with as much as the 'new rules'.

It is not generally known that the process of changing the rules started months before the February 12 IOC announcement. For the last half dozen years or so, many wrestling fans and competitors around the world had complained that the rules were too complex to follow and that a better solution than the 'ball draw', in particular, should be found to break scoreless ties. FILA's Rules Committee members were working with the national federations to make substantive changes when the IOC recommendation hastened the process.

The FILA Rules Committees consisted of the following individuals...

FREESTYLE	GRECO-ROMAN
Ahmed Ayik – Turkey	Csaba Hegedus – Hungary
Stan Dziedzic – USA	Mikhail Mamiashvili – Russia
Tomiaki Fukuda – Japan	Daulet Turlykhanov – Kazakhstan

Dziedzic takes a few minutes to explain the situation, "The process of fashioning a set of rules that were more dynamic, easier for the viewing public to understand and yet still allows for the best prepared to prevail began roughly a year ago, June 2012.

"The FILA Rules Working Group held a meeting last November 23 and 24 in

Budapest to discuss rule changes for the upcoming quadrennial. The group was comprised of the six gold medalists (three in Greco, three in freestyle) who have been elected onto the FILA Bureau; two officials; and a few statisticians/researchers. Unfortunately at the time, our President presented our groups with some false choices and limitations.

"After Lalovic and I met with the IOC's Christophe Dubi in March, we had a better understanding of the IOC's position and a broader platform as to potential rule changes. But some guiding principles remained — the rules should be simpler, modern, more dynamic and easier for the spectators to understand. Greco-Roman and freestyle must be made more distinguishable," said Dziedzic.

"Most important, the rules must ensure the best wrestlers prevail without even a hint of either duplicity or complicity. I hate the time when you can have the referee anoint the winner, ever. That's why I liked the idea that someone proposed to me regarding the 30-second warning — sort of like the shot clock. It assures us that we'll never have a tie — we'll never have the referees making the decision on declaring the winner.

"Each national federation — including USA Wrestling — was supplied a password for each discipline and urged to convene a forum for the fans, media and of course the wrestlers, to weigh in. From the results of these forums, each national federation was asked to construct and then submit its proposed set of rules."

It appears the U.S. could not come to an agreement on a common proposal so they submitted two proposed sets of rules.

Dziedzic explains, "Each U.S. proposal contained 'Technical Superiority' —one at eight to 10 points, the other at 15 points. One had a five-point throw and two three-point moves end the match if the wrestler had a higher score after the points were added. Only one suggested overtime, incorporating the following process: 'Flip a coin, the winner chooses offense or defense. If offense is chosen, he/she must score in one minute or the other wrestler wins the match. Just the opposite if he/she chooses defense.' One proposal wanted to 'bring passivity back in the game'; the other noted, 'We are not in favor of passivity but are in favor of fleeing the hold.' Fleeing the hold would be enforced under the current wrestling rule guidelines."

The FILA Vice-President offers his opinion about the IOC's position, "I think the IOC — and sometimes many coaches — want a flip of the coin because they don't trust the referees. The IOC understands in the relative scoring sports — gymnastics, diving, boxing — that there is an element of judgment. They want as much objective judgment as possible and they want the athletes as much as possible to make the decision. But they don't want chance; they don't want luck. So I think in the lesser of two evils — flipping a coin to determine who has to score or having a referee's judgment — the latter is preferred.

In the spring, the FILA Rules Committees reviewed all the proposals received from the national federations around the world.

"The 'new rules' were the result of a compilation of the proposals received from the federations, reflecting some compromises and a general consensus," said Dziedzic. "Allow me to make it clear — none of the suggestions are mine. Instead, they are the collective views of spectators, media and some of the best wrestlers and coaches in the world — past and present. My challenge was to sort through the countless recommendations and sculpt a simpler, more dynamic set of rules that are more modern, simpler and pleasing to the viewing audience."

The new rules were accepted by the FILA Extraordinary Congress delegates on May 18 in Moscow. The following day, at the United 4 Wrestling meet in Los

More than 20 Olympians met at the World Team Trials in Stillwater, Oklahoma to celebrate Olympic Day.

Angeles, the new rules were in play for the first time, including a 10-point margin for a technical fall in freestyle.

Opan Sat, a three-time European champion from Russia, said that while there was some confusion about how points were awarded, he was happy to be a part of a movement to save the sport. After winning two matches, Sat said through an interpreter, "I like the idea of having two periods because I have more time to execute my moves."

Jason Bryant, an editor at *Amateur Wrestling News* commented, "Less than 24 hours after the final senior-level international dual held in the United States concluded, there is actually a buzz about freestyle and Greco-Roman wrestling. Most, if not all, is centered around the new rules, reverting freestyle wrestling to a sport closer resembling the rules prior to 2005, when FILA came up with the oft-questioned, barely understandable three-period format."

In his column, Bryant quoted 2012 Olympic bronze medalist Coleman Scott as saying, "I like the rules, just watching the matches and being involved. There were a lot of points on the board and it looks good. Everyone was scrapping. The two-point takedown is a huge deal."

The women wrestlers liked the new rules as well. "I think the changes were great," said American wrestler Veronica Carlson, who competed in the Battle at the Falls women's wrestling event in Niagara Falls under the new rules. "You have to be more aggressive, which makes the matches more exciting."

"Cumulative scoring means you can wrestle your way back into the match," national 121-pound runner-up Katherine Fulp-Allen said. "That is why we saw a lot more takedowns, reversals and throws."

And the wrestling world went merrily along — until three weeks later, Friday, June 7 when FILA published the 42-page set of new rules on its website.

In the United States, the social media and internet message boards lit up with negative comments regarding some of the small-print details that were not widely known earlier. Comments such as, "These are not quite the same as what's been in use the past month or so. In particular, the tech-fall margin (described as 10 for freestyle and 7 for Greco) is actually 7 for both styles. In addition, a 5-point throw or two 3-point actions is also a tech-fall, provided the executor has the lead."

Jordan Burroughs was not so worried. He wrote on Facebook: "My take on wrestling's new rules. Don't get down by 7, don't get 5'd or taken down to your back 2x in the match. Sounds pretty simple to me. Why is everyone so bent out of shape? Hasn't the goal always been to score as many points as possible and give up as little as possible? ... The new rules are infinitely better now. A 5-point throw would always end the period and two 3-point moves as well. Why such a complaint now? Yes the matches are longer but there is such a level of difficulty to executing these moves that they should be rewarded."

It also should be noted that in the two international matches (the United 4 Wrestling and the Battle at the Falls) which were using the new rules with the 10-point tech fall margin, there were 14 freestyle matches where one wrestler moved out to a seven-point lead over his/her opponent. In no instance did the losing wrestler come from behind to win the match.

Dan Gable endorsed FILA's new rules: "The rules are definitely better," he said. "No more clinches or ball draws. I love having cumulative scoring and three-minute periods — that's what we needed. We've made really good progress in that area. The matches are more exciting and entertaining. There are still some tweaks and minor changes I think need to be made, but for the most part the rules are a lot better."

Rich Bender said: "The rules, well, I think they are a lot better today than they were on February 12. The fact that we have two three-minute periods, cumulative scoring and no ball-pull, those are positive changes that have been made. There are things I think we need to work on and tweak to make better. I'm not a fan of a five-point move ending a match, or two three-point moves ending a match. I'm a fan of overtime. I understand the rules, but I don't agree with all of them and a lot of Americans don't agree with all of them. Dziedzic and I have had several heated conversations about the rules.

"I think the tweaks they just made were in large part because of a one-day tournament at the World Championships. Going from a 10-point technical fall to a seven-point technical fall was done because of that. The freestyle recommendation originally was a 10-point tech. Guys might have to wrestle five matches in one day and a seven-point tech could shorten their day and shorten the tournament.

"I am glad they implemented the rules changes right away. I definitely agree with that decision. Our age groups (Juniors, Cadets) are going to stick with a 10-point technical fall; a five-pointer or two three-pointers won't end a match. I think they have it right. I think those are the best rules.

"I think FILA is listening more than they ever did before, and that's encouraging. Are the rules going to be perfect? Of course not. I don't think there is a perfect set of rules. For us, we would love the matches to be folkstyle, right? To say the rules suck, because you don't like a couple of the interpretations, I think is really doing a disservice to what's right with the rules."

Cornell University freshman Mark Grey appreciates the new rules. In an interview with *New York Wrestling News* while preparing to compete in the Junior World tournament in August, Grey remarked, "I love the new rules. Conditioning is a factor now. And I like the cumulative scoring. In the past, you basically had a two-minute sprint. Now, you can slowly wear guys down. Even if you give up some takedowns, if you keep going after guys, wearing them down, shots start to open up."

Along with all the online chatter regarding the new rules, there was significant discussion amongst USA Wrestling administrators, coaches and athletes regarding the rules to be used at the U.S. World Team Trials being held the weekend of June 21-22 in Stillwater, Oklahoma. Leading up to a regularly scheduled USA Wrestling Executive Committee teleconference on June 10, the athletes polled were in favor of one rule change — in cases of ties, rather than going to FILA's set of criteria for determining the winner, use sudden death overtime. Some have dubbed this as the Tucci Rule, since veteran international official Rick Tucci pushed hard for its inclusion.

The coaches and administrators were divided on the issue. Some feared that the overtime, particularly at the heaviest weights, might go on too long. (Some recalled the Greg Gibson-Bill Scherr finals bout lasting more than 15 minutes of overtime back in the 1980s.) Some were in favor of setting a time limit to overtime; if no score after three minutes, then go to criteria. Others were worried that hours of wrestling might be added on to already long days. It was noted that 70% of the matches in the London Olympics ended in two periods or less (four minutes). Would the new rules shorten or lengthen matches overall?

Within USA Wrestling, the Greco-Roman Sports Committee and the Women's Sports Committee agreed to use the existing FILA criteria for determining the winner of a match that is tied at the end of regulation. The Freestyle Sports Committee decided that the men's freestyle matches that ended in a draw would go to sudden-death overtime with no time limit. The USA Wrestling Executive Committee approved those recommendations. Thus, two sets of rules would be used and would give the administrators, wrestlers, coaches and fans an interesting look at both solutions.

The Greco-Roman folks in the U.S. were more positive about the new rules than their freestyle counterparts. From an article written by Bryce Miller in the *Des Moines Register*, USA Wrestling Greco-Roman coach Steve Fraser was quoted, "In general, we love the new rules. Love them. Love them. Old rules actually destroyed a lot of incentive to score. It's very, very positive," said Fraser. "Everybody in the United States I've talked to — and I'm sure around the world, based on a conversations I've had with my coach friends from foreign countries — are really happy. This is a drastic change, and it's needed."

Fraser said rule changes that now will penalize a wrestler for keeping his head down or grabbing hands to limit action undoubtedly will benefit Greco-Roman long-term, as well. "People will be forced to engage chest to chest in the old Greco-Roman tradition," he said. "That's a good thing. It brings back conditioning, it brings back endurance, which has always been a U.S. asset.

"Greco-Roman is trying more to use passivity to spur activity. It includes a '3 [passivity calls] and out' rule."

Shortly after the new rules were published, both the Russia and the U.S. held their World Championship Team Trials. In addition, wrestling was featured in the Mediterranean Games in Turkey. Cracks in FILA unity were evident, as tournament officials in all three cases deviated from the published rules. The Russians wrestled under the old 'one-point' takedown rule; the American freestylers used unlimited overtime to declare the winner of a bout ending in a tie; and, inexplicitly, the Mediterranean Games were wrestled completely under the old set of rules.

The Americans and the Russians expressed different opinions on several of the rules. The Russians liked the seven-point technical fall and the five-point and two three-point moves that end the match. They did not endorse the two-point award for the takedown. Essentially, the Russians place more emphasis on turns than takedowns for scoring points and felt that the two-point takedown devalued the importance of turns and higher-risk moves.

Two-time Olympic champion Sergei Beloglazov voiced his preference for one-point takedowns. Below is an excerpt from that interview. The translation is from Google.

Veteran international wrestling official Rick Tucci hopes that the rules become more standardized starting in 2014.

Q. In the championship of Russia takedowns will be worth just one point, yet by the rules of FILA — two points. What is the best?

A. Beloglazov: Definitely one point. Russia's entire coaching body endorses the one-point valuation. Otherwise just depreciate full two and three scoring action. The first day of the championship of Russia showed that with one point for takedowns contractions got very efficient.

In the men's U.S. World Team Trials, of the 14 freestyle finals matches, there was one fall, three technical falls and one overtime bout. While there were no major problems, some controversy arose over several aspects of the rules.

The unlimited overtime modification instituted by USA Wrestling sparked controversy when Kyle Dake and Andrew Howe wrestled in excess of six minutes of overtime in the challenge round final before Dake finally secured the winning takedown. Both of the exhausted wrestlers lost their next match by technical fall in less than two minutes. A coincidence? Hardly…

Few seemed to embrace the rule where two three-point moves ended the match. For instance, as reported by Jason Bryant on his wrestling blog, "…the challenge tournament final at 60kg Jimmy Kennedy and Nick Simmons put 20 points on the board in the first three minutes. Kennedy's 3-pointer at the end of the first period served as his second 3-point move, ending the match, robbing the spectators of another three minutes of high-level, high-energy wrestling."

As one might expect, 2011 World Team member Simmons did not speak well of the two three-point rule, "That rule is pretty ridiculous. I love the cumulative scoring and all the risks that wrestlers are taking now. I think it's great and that's one of the reasons I came back to wrestle here. They just need to change that rule with the two three-pointers."

Tucci, a member of the FILA Rules Commission for 20 years, likes the new rules overall but is leery that some modifications being made during the summer are making things more complex for the spectator to understand and putting more judgment into the hands of the official — "all things the IOC doesn't want to see in wrestling," he claims. He grimaces at the one-point counter-takedown rule that was in effect in early August at the women's freestyle Trials in Colorado Springs and later at the Cadet and Junior World Championships.

Tucci figures, "All takedowns equal two points — that's simple: for the spectators, the contestants, the officials. Until the World Championships in Budapest are over, there will be confusion about the rules, but after that I hope that FILA says, 'Here are the standard rules for wrestling; everyone will use these for the next four years.'"

In late July in Fargo, USA Wrestling sponsored the ASICS/Vaughan Cadet and Junior National championships. Billed as the largest wrestling tournament in the world, a modified version of FILA rules were in place. The significant modifications included: a wrestler needed to have a 10-point, not a seven-point, lead to secure a technical fall; also, the officials ignored awarding a technical fall to a wrestler with two three-point or one five-point move. Officials generally appeared pleased with these modifications for the younger athletes.

Dziedzic sums things up, "The challenge was to find the balance — number of points needed to provide an incentive for the better wrestler to expend the energy to reach it, yet doesn't short change the viewing audience of action.

"A large number of the better wrestlers indicated the differential is a function of time between matches. In a one-day format where the time between the quarter-finals and semi-finals may be as short as 15 minutes, the best wrestlers said: when I reach the 5-0 lead I might seek two more points, but not five more. If you set the differential at 10 points, you will deprive the fans of action, as most will conserve energy and skip seeking a technical fall.

"If a two-day format is used — especially if the repechage includes the loser to the quarter-finals, and the semi-finals are wrestled the next day — a 10-point differential is more feasible. A wrestler in the hotly contested quarter-finals may seek the 10-point technical fall since he has a day to rest and wants to go the sauna to make weight. The fans and the best wrestlers are in harmony.

"We can put these rules into effect this year, take a look at them and at the end of the year we can always massage them," he concluded.

Asked if the 2013 World Championships in Budapest would be wrestled under the recently published FILA rules, a FILA official replied, "That's the way it's supposed to happen."

CHAPTER 21 / **Fargo Dreams**

MANY OF the current Senior level athletes' competitive careers will not be directly affected if wrestling is missing from the Olympic program in 2020 and beyond. They will already have made their challenges for the right to represent the USA in the 2012 Games in London and the 2016 Games in Rio.

The ones most likely affected will be those individuals who are now in their teens and younger — Cadet and Junior level wrestlers working their way up the national rankings. More than 4100 such youth wrestlers across seven divisions competed in the annual Fargo Nationals at North Dakota State University during the week of July 13, 2013. One of the more outstanding wrestlers in the tournament tells about his Olympic hopes and fears.

Adam Coon's athletic dream was launched when he was very young. Coon sat in front of the television as a wide-eyed five-year-old when a pudgy, unheralded American heavyweight stepped on the mat to face a chiseled Russian legend in the 2000 Olympic finals. Coon watched excitedly as Rulon Gardner shocked the world by knocking off three-time Olympic champion Alexander Karelin to win the Olympic gold medal in Sydney, Australia.

"It was awesome to see Rulon win the Olympics," Coon said. "He was the heavyweight who was a farm boy who took down the Russian monster. Rulon Gardner was an idol and a hero to me growing up. I wanted to be like him and I wanted to win an Olympic gold medal like he did. He definitely inspired me."

The 18-year-old Coon's Olympic dream received a jolt on February 12 when the IOC Executive Board recommended wrestling be removed as a core sport on the Olympic program.

"I saw a link about it on Facebook that day and I just couldn't believe it," said Coon. "My initial reaction was that I was just shocked. I don't think anybody thought that wrestling was going to be taken out of the Olympics. Wrestling was one of the original Olympic sports. I had a lot of questions running through my head. I wondered why they could even think about taking it out. It just didn't make any sense."

Coon, an honor student from Fowlerville, Michigan, became the first wrestler to capture back-to-back USA Wrestling Triple Crowns at the Junior level. He dominated the competition at 285 pounds in the Greco-Roman and freestyle tournaments in Fargo, putting his immense strength and power on full display. Coon also has thought about how he would be impacted if wrestling is taken out of the Olympics.

"You obviously hope that wrestling stays in the Olympics, but we may only have one shot in 2016," said Coon, who won a FILA Cadet World title in 2011. "That could really be crunch time for a lot of younger guys like me. We may only have one opportunity, and we may not have that time to mature for 2020 and 2024 like we thought we would. Hopefully, the International Olympic Committee will keep wrestling in so we can have a shot to make those teams when we're hitting our peak as wrestlers."

Coon is one of many aspiring hopefuls — along with young stars like California's Aaron Pico, Hawaii's Teshya Alo and Colorado's Mark Hall — who project as wrestlers who could make U.S. Olympic teams in wrestling in 2020 and 2024. All four excelled at the ASICS/Vaughan 2013 National Championships in Fargo.

Like Coon, Pico is a special young talent who also is highly skilled and very mature for his age. Although just 16 years old, Pico may be one of the top American prospects since 2008 Olympic gold medalist Henry Cejudo. Pico competed admirably at the FILA Cadet World Championships in August, bringing home the only Cadet gold medal for the USA.

"Pico's actually thinking 2016 Olympics, and he's been thinking it for a couple of years," U.S. Assistant National Coach Bill Zadick said. "He's only 16, but would you say Pico's at the level Henry Cejudo was at that age? Yes, he probably is.

"2016 is certainly a tall order, but it's not unrealistic for a kid like Aaron Pico. He's good, but he obviously still has a long way to go to get to that level. What I love about him is that he has the right attitude, and he's very open-minded about growing and improving as a wrestler."

Pico is just a high school sophomore from Whittier, California where he is coached in the international style of wrestling by the Ukrainian, Valentin Kalika. He is already thinking along the same lines that Cejudo did in the years before

Adam Coon, the Fargo champion at 285 pounds in both Greco and Freestyle in 2013, will wrestle collegiately for the University of Michigan.
John Sachs

Aaron Pico will be trying to replicate the effort of 2008 Olympian Henry Cejudo, who won an Olympic gold medal right out of high school. T.R. Foley

the young Californian won his Olympic gold in 2008. You don't hear Pico talking about going to college or any goals regarding NCAA championships. Instead, he is focused on training and competing globally in freestyle.

After his victorious Cadet World championship bout at 63kg, Pico said, "This is the first big step for me on the international level. I want to keep progressing and win world titles at the Junior and Senior levels. Obviously, the ultimate goal for me is winning an Olympic gold medal. Hopefully, I will be able to pursue that goal in 2016 and beyond."

The 15-year-old Alo rolled to Junior and Cadet National titles this past July in Fargo. She repeated as Cadet National champion; was named Outstanding Wres-

Teshya Alo, a Hawaiian who excels in judo and wrestling, earned a bronze medal in the Cadet World championships this past summer. John Sachs

tler of the Cadet tournament; and, won the Junior 125 pound championship with a first period fall. She later went on to win a bronze medal at the Cadet World Championships in August.

Alo also is accomplished as a national champion in judo. She is a very talented wrestler with the type of ability that could translate to an Olympic medal someday. She has some unique Olympic dreams. "I want to compete in the Olympics in both wrestling and judo," said Alo, from Honolulu, Hawaii. "I know it would be difficult, but my goal is to win an Olympic medal in both sports."

Alo's parents both wrestled in high school, and she began wrestling at age seven. She started competing in judo a year later. "The Olympics have been my goal since I won my first national title in wrestling," Alo said. "I was nine years old, and it's been my dream ever since."

Alo is the best prospect coming out of Hawaii since Olympic bronze medalist and World champion Clarissa Chun. Chun is now helping coach Alo. Chun placed

Mark Hall, just 16 years young, has already spent considerable time wrestling at the U.S. Olympic Training Center. John Sachs

fifth in the 2008 Olympics before earning a bronze medal at the 2012 Olympics.

"Clarissa inspired me when she won a medal at the Olympics," Alo said. "It was great to see her running around the mat holding up the American flag after she won her medal. Clarissa did a really good job. She is super fast and strong. She has a judo background like I do, so I can learn a lot from her."

Alo also has studied Olympic and World champion wrestler Jordan Burroughs. "I love his doubles, because that's what I do now," she said. "My coaches tell me not to shoot my doubles from my knees, but then I pop up a video on YouTube of Jordan Burroughs. You see him shooting a blast double from his knees and scoring takedowns with it."

Alo is optimistic wrestling will stay in the Olympics. "I'm a little nervous about the vote in September, but I'm more excited because I think they will keep wrestling in the Olympics," she said. "I'm very hopeful I will have a chance to wrestle in the Olympics some day. I want to win an Olympic gold medal. That's what I'm shooting for."

Hall is another gifted wrestler who is very advanced for a 16-year-old. He's already spent considerable time at the U.S. Olympic Training Center in Colorado Springs. Before heading to Fargo, he lined up for a match at an OTC practice against Olympian Haislan Garcia of Canada. Garcia placed fifth in the 2010 World Championships.

Hall completed an amazing run through the Fargo field culminated by shutting out Kamal Bey of Illinois 10-0 in the 160-pound finals. He did not allow a point in the tournament.

"I've been training out at the Olympic Training Center since April and I've been getting my butt kicked a lot," Hall said. "I've improved during the time I've been in Colorado Springs and that has helped me a lot up here. I just came out and was looking to dominate in my matches."

Coon has thrived in wrestling while also excelling in football and track and field. He had numerous offers from NCAA Division I schools to play college football, but he instead chose to wrestle for the University of Michigan.

Even with wrestling's Olympic fate still uncertain, Coon is not second-guessing his decision to wrestle in college. "I love football, but I've been wrestling since I was five years old," he said. "I have so many more goals and dreams in wrestling. I am very passionate about wrestling — I always have been. Nothing is going to change that."

Coon, like many top young prospects his age, is trying to stay optimistic about wrestling's Olympic future.

"I've had a goal since I was very young to be up on that podium and to win an Olympic medal," Coon said. "It's a huge dream of mine to be an Olympic champion. It would be really unfortunate if they take that opportunity away from us."

CHAPTER 22 / **Olympia's Hallowed Grounds**

"Today I became the first woman to ever wrestle on the Ancient Olympic grounds where wrestlers competed so many years ago. As a Greek-American, it was a tremendous honor to be a part of this event. Losing was upsetting, but learning about the history of the Olympics and about the purpose for its establishment gave me new insights into what and why I do what I do. Wrestling is character building and this loss challenges me and helps me to grow as an athlete and a person." — From Helen Maroulis's Facebook page, July 21, 2013

WRESTLING trivia buffs will tell you that the greatest Olympic wrestler was not named Baumgartner or Smith, or Karelin, or Medved, or Saitiev, or Beloglazov or Yoshida. It was Milo of Croton. Milo was a six-time Olympic champion. He reportedly first won the boy's championship and later earned five men's Olympic wrestling titles between 536 and 520 BC. He wrestled those matches at the home of the Olympic Movement — on the sands of the Palestra courtyard in Olympus, Greece, 200 miles southwest of Athens. The Palestra was a school building devoted to the training of Greek wrestlers and boxers. Since the Ancient Games were curtailed in 394 AD, it is believed that no sporting event has ever been held on the hallowed grounds where Milo prevailed over 2,500 years ago.

Until July 20 and 21, 2013, that is.

Supporters of wrestling's argument to remain as an Olympic event will often point to the historic impact of the sport in Olympic annals. FILA states that the first real traces of the development of wrestling date back to the times of the Sumerians, 5000 years ago. The sport made its ancient Olympic Games introduction at the

Milo was one tough Greek warrior.

The wrestling event at Olympus was the brainchild of USA Wrestling's Harris Kalofonos and was considered a huge success, gaining worldwide publicity for the sport.

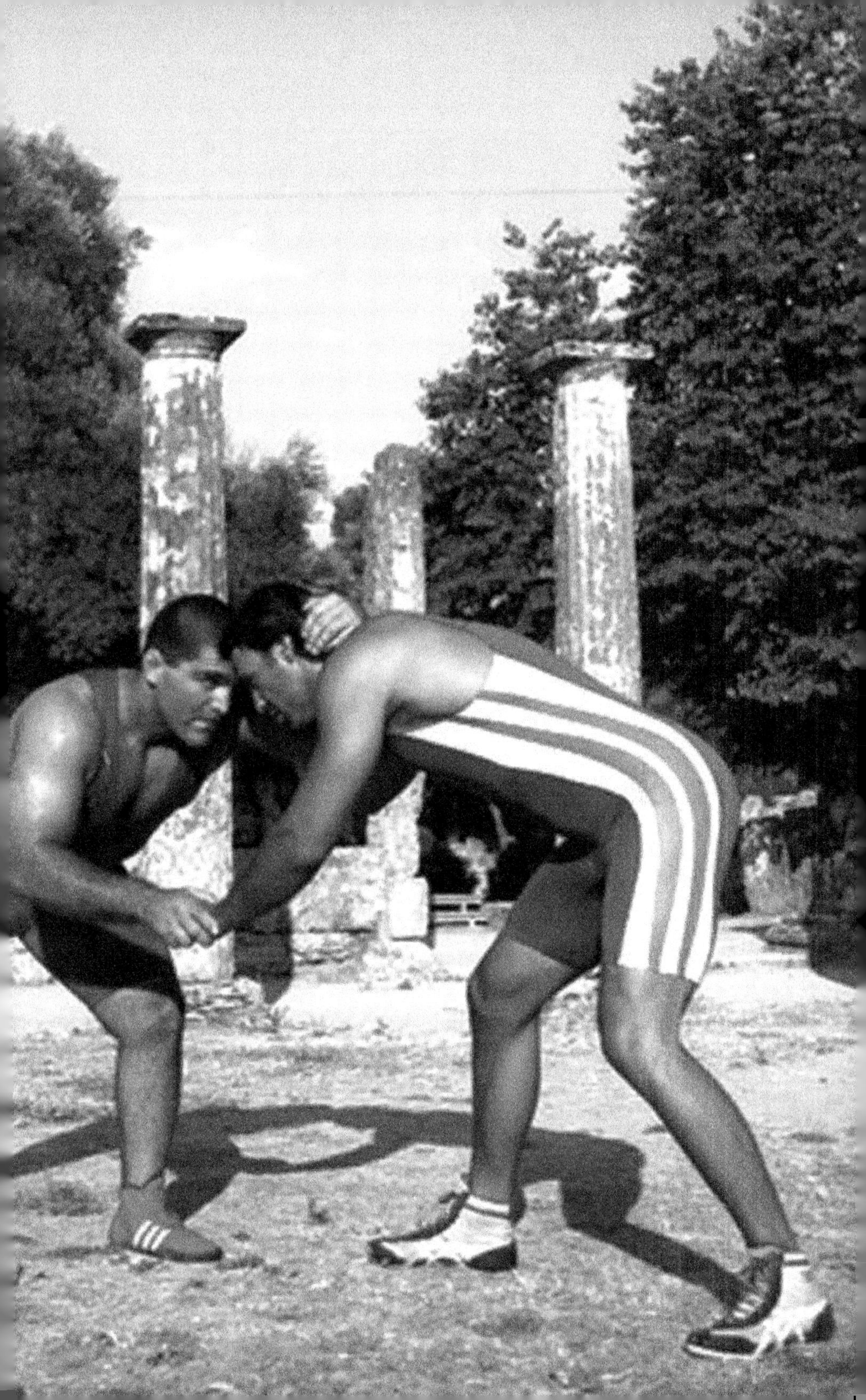

Several members of the USA women's team enjoyed posing for the Take a Stance promotion while at Olympia.

18th Olympiad in 708 BC. It stayed as a pillar of the program for 273 Games until Emperor Theodosius decreed that all such "pagan cults" be banned.

Greco-Roman wrestling returned as part of the first modern Olympic program in 1896. Squash and baseball/softball can make no such claims. How to best leverage this advantage was a question on FILA's mind for months.

Right after the IOC vote in February, Harris Kalofonos on USA Wrestling's staff in Colorado Springs concocted the brilliant idea to actively exploit the sport's historical advantage...

• Let's stage the Olympia Tournament, already somewhat of an annual fixture on the international wrestling calendar, on the site of wrestling's Grecian origins.

Wrestling is a world-wide sport for all people and all ages as demonstrated by these two young girls at the Olympia wrestling meet.

• Let's invite the global media to cover these matches in a most unique, symbolic setting.

• Let's show the world that wrestling is returning to its roots and that it cannot be forgotten or dismissed.

• Let's stage an international tournament at the same place where Milo of Croton won his medals!

Once the wrestling delegation won the shortlist vote in May in St. Petersburg, CPOW's Bill Scherr started pushing for and supporting the Olympus idea.

Now, you just don't go to the Olympia web page and look to see if there are any other events taking place at the site of the original Olympics during a summer weekend and sign up for one of the available spots. Once the idea was approved USA Wrestling and FILA turned to Kalofonos. He returned to his native Greece for a few weeks, where he met with the authorities, including the Greek Olympic Committee and the Greek government officials. It appears that Kalofonos, FILA and the Greek Wrestling Federation president Constantine Thanos used a few silver bullets (metaphorically speaking, of course) with the Greek authorities to gain their approval to wrestle the tournament on the sacred grounds.

Kalofonos passed the credit around. He said, "None of this would have been possible without the leadership of the International Olympic Academy that is based in ancient Olympia. Dionisis Gangas, director of the Academy, played a big role in making the event happen."

Succeed they did. The government of Greece gave their permission and 11 nations from South America, North America, Europe and Asia agreed to participate in the two-day event on the third weekend in July.

Once again, thanks to the public relations efforts of CPOW and FILA, the international press corps was all over the festivities. Gary Abbott stated, "The Olympia event was the biggest public relations boost for wrestling in Phase Two, at a time when the other two sports were very quiet. It was a huge success for wrestling."

The first day of the tournament, Saturday, July 20, was devoted to youth wrestling exhibitions and the early rounds of the men's and women's competition. FILA President Nenad Lalovic was present, greeting contestants, spectators and the press. He was not oblivious to the surroundings and the youngsters practicing in their singlets amongst the Greek ruins.

In a FILA press release, Lalovic exclaimed, "These youth, and many more like them around the world, dream of wrestling in the Olympic Games and we are doing everything we can to ensure they have that opportunity."

The tournament was not held inside the ancient stadium of Olympia. The matches took place on the grounds of the International Olympic Academy which the IOC established in 1961 to promote the Olympic ideals. Saturday's contests were staged indoors in a modern gymnasium to protect the athletes from the conditions.

Sunday's finals matches for all weight classes and styles were held in the evening; these were the only outdoor events. In its endeavor to optimize its public relations outreach, FILA live-streamed the showcase event on its official Facebook page. Cameramen were able to capture not just the wrestlers, but many of the spectators in the crowd sporting signs and shirts with the #SaveOlympicWrestling motto dotting the historic landscape.

The competition at Olympus included men's and women's freestyle and men's Greco-Roman matches. The host country Greeks dominated the Greco-Roman portion of the tournament, winning five of the seven weight classes. Americans Ellis Coleman and Geordan Speiller won the two remaining weights. Russia took control of the freestyle medals, winning six of the seven golds. There were no finalists from the two-person USA squad.

Women's freestyle competition saw four American wrestlers in the finals. Alyssa Lampe handily won the 48kg weight class, but Helen Maroulis, Elena Pirozhkova, and Tamyra Mensah all lost to their Russian opponents and had to settle for silver medals.

Maroulis talked enthusiastically about her weekend. "Wrestling at Olympia was an incredible experience. The first day we wrestled in a gym across the street from the original site. On Sunday they provided us with a tour guide before the matches. We got to walk all around the Palestra and the old Olympic sites and we learned all about the history of the Olympics.

"Not that much has changed since then, except — back in those days, the Games were for men only; women were not permitted to even watch.

"The men wrestled naked. Do you know why?"

Maroulis answered her own question. "Well, the Games were intended to honor the gods. In every way that man competed, he needed to have a good body. Those who trained the hardest usually had the best bodies. So, the athletes wanted to show off these great bodies to the gods. There was no hiding behind clothes."

Maroulis continued, "For the finals that evening we wrestled on the site up the hill from the Palestra. There was just one mat which was set up outdoors. It was hot at the start; later on it cooled down but because of an accumulation of dew, the mat became quite slippery.

"While it may not have been the best of wrestling conditions, it was still such a memorable event," said Maroulis. "There was lots of pageantry. The FILA president was there, many Greece officials, the mayor of Olympia, lots of press corps. I'll never forget it."

Maroulis concluded, "I believe that the event gave wrestling a huge boost in showing the world about its roots from thousands of years ago. Wrestling is for everyone. I want to see wrestling in the Olympics not just for me but for all the wrestlers worldwide. Wrestling builds such great moral character and good values. If wrestling is not part of the Olympics there will be bad effects globally. People may not have the opportunity to develop those characteristics if the sport is not around."

Veteran sports writer David Owen summed the weekend up well in an article found on Facebook: "In a sports movement defined by its ancient heritage, the history card played at Olympia by a sport that has been on the Olympic programme since 708 BC is an ace, trump and joker rolled into one."

CHAPTER 23 / **The Dog Days of Summer**

THE TERM 'Dog Days of Summer' is nearly as old as wrestling itself. Historians trace its origin back to the ancient Greeks, though it was the Romans who are given credit for naming those hot summer months of July and August after the brightest star in the night sky, Sirius, or the Dog Star. The Dog Days originally were those days when Sirius rose just before or at the same time as sunrise. The Romans sacrificed a red dog to appease the rage of Sirius, believing that the star was the cause of the sultry weather. Dog Days were popularly thought to be an evil time.

During the Dog Days of 2013, members of FILA and CPOW were sacrificing all their free hours and then some, as they made and executed plans to avoid future evil times – those years after 2016 when potentially the world exists without wrestling as an Olympic sport.

Nenad Lalovic continued to provide the kind of leadership that had been lacking for years at the international wrestling level. He was earning the praise and respect of those inside and outside the wrestling community. Serving as the face of wrestling, Lalovic travelled the world, meeting with FILA delegates, IOC members, athletic commissions, heads of state and the many media contacts that Bob Condron set up for him. He kept his FILA Bureau constituency updated as to the progress being made to win the IOC vote on September 8, as this letter demonstrates...

Corsier, 15 July 2013
Dear Bureau Members,
I am writing to you to provide an overview of the work that is in progress to support FILA's campaign to regain our position on the Olympic Program.

As you know we were successful at the IOC Executive Board in St. Petersburg. In the first round of voting, wrestling was decisively selected as one of three sports to be put forward to the IOC session for consideration. After the multiple rounds of voting that then followed, squash and baseball/ softball were selected as the other two sports to be considered.

However, this was just the beginning of our work and much needs to be done and is being done to bring wrestling back to the Olympic Games.

This is not something that can be managed only with our internal human resources and I have appointed a team of experts who between them have vast experience working for cities bidding for the Olympic Games and working on behalf of sports bidding to join the Olympic Program. Included are experts on:

- *International Relations*
- *Public Relations*
- *Marketing*
- *Creative services for our final presentation to be given at the IOC session*

As a part of our international relations work, as your President I have represented FILA at major Olympic Family meetings in order to meet with IOC members and to build support for our sport (SportAccord, ASOIF, ANOC, IOC Session in Lausanne, Mediterranean Games, University Games).

At events that I have not been able to attend personally, I have greatly appreciated the support of key members of the Bureau and others who have represented FILA on my behalf (Singapore Athletes Commission, Abidjan ANOCA).

Many Bureau Members offered their good services to help FILA in its struggle by contacting IOC persons of influence such as Messrs. Pellicane, Fukuda, Dziedzic, Tarkong, Jim Scherr, Gama Filho, Mamiashvili, Karelin, Dr. Kim, Hamakos, Tzenov, Hegedus, Ayik, Mrs. Yaksi.

However, time is limited and consequently we have implemented other programs designed to reach out to the IOC membership. This includes the direct support of our NFs with certain IOC members. We also have to respect the IOC Rules of Conduct for bidding sports.

On the public relations side, FILA has befitted from a vast increase in media coverage. In the early stages some of this was inevitable as a result of the exclusion of wrestling by the IOC. However, our PR advisors have provided FILA with a strong and positive platform to communicate with the Olympic Movement and other interest groups. We are doing this through traditional PR activities and also through social media.

Our final presentation at the IOC Session will be an important part of the campaign. Our presentation team that met with the IOC Executive Board in St. Peters-

burg made a strong impression and will be the core of our team at the IOC Session. Our advisors are already starting to produce speeches and films that will set out wrestling's core propositions to the IOC membership. Professional presentation training will be included in our preparations.

I hope that the above provides a good overview of our campaign. There remains much work to do and I may call on the direct support of our Bureau members from time to time.

I would like each of you to call me by phone if you have any good contacts with IOC members and we can discuss how to proceed in accordance with our and your informations.

Our strength comes from the ethos of our sport. We are determined and relentless in our efforts to return our great sport to the Olympic Program.

Yours sincerely,
Nenad Lalovic FILA President

One problem that wrestling knew they had to attack before the Buenos Aires vote was television. It was well understood that the IOC were concerned about the apparant drop in broadcast ratings that wrestling received during the last several Olympics.

FILA sent Karl-Martin Dittmann, general secretary of the German Wrestling Federation, to meet with executives from the Olympic Broadcasting Services (OBS) at their headquarters in Madrid, Spain. The OBS is the host broadcaster for all of the Olympic events. Dittmann explained some of the changes being made in wrestling such as increased scoring and spectacular throws which will make the sport more entertaining for the viewer. He was particularly interested in exchanging ideas with the production specialists in ways to improve the presentation of the sport to the viewing public.

The parties agreed that for the 2016 Olympics they would use modern technology to enhance the experience of television audiences. Ideas include experimenting with the use of additional cameras, potentially one on the referee. They also discussed presenting real-time biometrics data on the screen during the contests.

After the Madrid session, Insidethegames.biz reported Lalovic's favorable reaction to the meeting: "FILA appreciated the opportunity to meet with the television experts at OBS and to learn from their experience," said the Serbian. "The advice that has been provided will help us to better serve the needs of broadcasters and to provide a more attractive and exciting presentation of our sport to TV audiences around the world.

"Just as we have modernised our rules, we must explore innovative ways in which we can better present our sport to a wide audience. We've got a great sport, but we must embrace new technologies, new presentations and let the world see the unique aspects of wrestling."

In a bit of a surprise move during the summer months, FILA went on the offensive by increasing significantly its budget for out-of-competition anti-doping tests. Although doping has not been viewed as much of a problem in international wrestling, Lalovic wanted to make sure that it did not become one. Reportedly, he raised the budget by five times its previous amount of funding.

FILA, indeed, was implementing many changes to improve the sport since the February 12 vote. One of Lalovic's main goals during the dog days was to make sure that every one of the 103 members of the IOC General Assembly — the voters on September 8 — were well informed about the positively received changes that wrestling was making. The international sport of wrestling was no longer the dreary, difficult-to-understand combat event that was given the heave-ho by the IOC Executive Board back in February. It was imperative that every voter understood this.

While many of the IOC general assembly voters had been contacted in the spring and early summer by Lalovic, Dziedzic, the Scherrs and others, there was still more than a handful or two that had not been contacted about wrestling's new look. Lalovic reached out to national federation leaders around the world to contact certain IOC members in their home countries. Send an email; write a letter (Lalovic's office supplied a sample); make a phone call; plan a personal visit — that was the charge to wrestling's 177 national federation groups. September 8 was fast approaching and the Serbian president wanted to make sure that every IOC member knew that FILA cared about them – and their support.

Lalovic himself was very comfortable playing the role of wrestling's chief ambassador to the IOC and the world. It was reported by the Asahi Shibum GLOBE that at the extraordinary session of the IOC held in early July in Lausanne, the FILA President "has wrestled a few people to the bar to regale them in five languages about why his sport deserves a place."

During the dog days Lalovic could be found most everywhere a group of IOC members were congregating. A highlight was the World Track and Field Championships in Moscow in mid-August. Accompanied by Andrew Craig and Jim Scherr, Lalovic met approximately 35 IOC members in a relaxed setting.

His travels were further highlighted by an appearance at the United Nations once again where he was an invited guest of Jacques Rogge at a luncheon the IOC President was hosting on August 23. The luncheon followed the session of proclamation of the International Day of Sport at the United Nations General Assembly.

From there the FILA President headed to Rio de Janeiro for the Judo World Championships the last week in August.

Meanwhile, positive signs for wrestling's Olympic future were making news. A leading candidate to become to next IOC President in September, Germany's Thomas Bach, made the following remarks in a speech to the Foreign Press Association in Berlin, "I have the impression that the international federation (FILA) has understood very well the messages sent to them. The international federation has drawn its conclusions. It is now here with a new president, new programme and new ideas for the sport," said Bach. "That is why I personally believe that wrestling has good chances to come through the vote in September."

Another IOC presidential candidate, Ukraine's Sergey Bubka, publically spoke about the positive moves that wrestling has made, saying, "In a really short period [FILA has] made fantastic progress," Bubka said. "They've made a lot of changes regarding the rules and women's participation, regarding the ethical issues. I think this is a very positive change."

And Switzerland's Denis Oswald, also in the running for IOC President, announced that he would be voting for wrestling in Buenos Aires. He labeled the IOC Board's recommendation in February as a "mistake" — one that needs to be corrected

Stan Dziedzic was encouraged by these statements — along with feedback that he was receiving from several other IOC presidential candidates. In a July 31 email to some wrestling supporters, Dziedzic wrote in an email: "I believe Bach, Carrion, Bubka and Oswald (all of whom are announced candidates to replace Rogge as IOC President) harbor similar feelings — in that order. It's good the Presidential elections are a day after the vote for the inclusion of the one spot for 2020 and 2024. It should keep the other candidates from opposing this view, unless of course it would be deemed to be helpful to their election chances, which in my view is not the case.

"If one of the above is elected, I hope he will reshape the debate — less on the # of sports and more towards the total # of athletes. Eventually, the distinction between core and adjunct may be removed."

Dan Gable offered his thoughts: "Wrestling is the greatest sport there is and one of the most demanding sports there is," he said. "I'm very passionate about the sport. I'm always trying to keep people motivated and inspired about wrestling. We need to get the sport back in the Olympics and then continue to improve the sport after that."

Gable had mixed emotions just over a month before the September 8 vote. "Am I a little bit nervous about the vote? Yes, I'm nervous because there are a lot of

FILA has high hopes that new IOC President Thomas Bach will work closely with wrestling to restore it as a 'core' Olympic sport.

politics involved," he said. "And who really knows exactly what the IOC members are thinking. I do feel really good about wrestling's history in the Olympics and I feel really good about how wrestling has stepped up since February 12. We've done a lot of great things and made a lot of great changes. Wrestling has the sentimentality of people in the world now because of what we've done. It would be a shame if wrestling is taken out of the Olympics. We need to do everything we can to make sure that doesn't happen."

An ongoing CPOW and FILA social media campaign to interactively communicate to the world those positive changes that wrestling was making hit high gear during the dog days. Having launched a Keep Wrestling in the Olympics Facebook page shortly after the February IOC recommendation, by the end of August the USA Wrestling developed page had gained more than 116,000 likes worldwide.

FILA had less than 1,000 likes on its Facebook page in February. The number of likes had grown to close to 100,000 as the final September 8 vote drew near.

USA Wrestling also helped launch a Keep Wrestling in the Olympics Twitter page in February. That page, the official Twitter of the U.S.-based CPOW had 13,000-plus followers in August. FILA's Olympic Wrestling Twitter site, also launched in February, had more than 44,000 followers by the end of August 2013.

The Take A Stance initiative, started in August by USA Wrestling and FILA, encouraged people from around the world to submit photos while getting into wrestling stances in interesting locations to show their support for the Olympic fight. Among the top wrestlers taking part were Olympic gold medalists Saori Yoshida and Kaori Icho of Japan, along with Olympic medalists Carol Huynh and Tonya Verbeek of Canada. Take A Stance photos were submitted and posted from landmarks like the Great Wall of China, the Eiffel Tower, Buckingham Palace, the U.S. Capitol, the Washington Monument, Times Square, the Statue of Liberty and Pikes Peak.

USA Wrestling also started a weekly Google+ Hangout Series where athletes, media and fans have gathered on video to discuss important issues involved with keeping wrestling in the Olympics. Top wrestlers that have taken part in the Google+ Hangout Series include Rulon Gardner, Jordan Burroughs, Daniel Igali, Kyle Dake, Clarissa Chun, Jessica MacDonald, and Helen Maroulis.

"Social media has played a pivotal role in the fight to keep wrestling in the Olympics," said Richard Immel, social media coordinator for USA Wrestling. "It is a truly unique experience that provides the ordinary person not in a position of power the opportunity to be heard. Utilizing social media platforms, the leaders of wrestling have been able to spread important information in fast time to those who want to see it. The wrestling community has galvanized and has an army behind it ready and willing to go to battle for this sport."

Immel's partner on the social media committee was Patrick Wixted from Ketchum. Gary Abbott had high praise for Wixted: "Patrick has been involved in every level of decisions on the PR side. He set up our conference calls from St. Petersburg, organized the clip service we do, and consulted on pretty much everything. He was the go-to person for Ketchum, and organized pulling in other assets from their staff into all our projects."

Complimenting Wixted was Ketchum's Joe Favorito, a pitch-man extraordinaire who helped land many of the national and international interviews Ketchum set up for CPOW. Considered a legend in the business, he also was the key person in getting so many national and international media to the Rumble on the Rails

During a CPOW conference call on August 3, members on the call were in an optimistic but cautious mood. Jim Scherr suggested that wrestling was at this point the frontrunner to win the IOC vote in September. He thought that wrestling had up to 40 confirmed votes within the IOC general assembly, with another dozen or so maybes.

Scherr announced that the same five-person team that made the presentation in St. Petersburg in May would be making the September IOC presentation. The

THE DOG DAYS OF SUMMER

BUCKINGHAM PALACE

18th July, 2013

Dear Mr Nicholson,

The Princess Royal has asked me to thank you and Malcolm Morley for your recent letters concerning British Wrestling and its involvement in the Olympic Movement. Her Royal Highness is grateful to you for taking the trouble to write and rest assured she is well aware of the strength of opinion that supports Wrestling for inclusion in the Olympic programme.

Thank you again for taking the trouble to write.

Yours sincerely,
Nick Wright

Captain Nick Wright, CVO, Royal Navy
Private Secretary to
HRH The Princess Royal

Colin Nicholson, Esq.

Great Britain's Princess Royal, an IOC member, responds to FILA's approach. The organization mounted an extraordinary PR campaign that eventually reaped the benefits of a great deal of hard work and ingenuity.

group was planning on showing two videos during their 20-minute time allowance; one video would be completely new, and one video that was shown before would be enhanced.

The CPOW group touched upon the subject of the future of wrestling after September 8 and overall finances. John Bardis led the discussion about CPOW continuing to lead changes in the sport especially in regards to gender equity. He was encouraging CPOW to assume a leadership role in working to build women's wrestling programs in the U.S. at the college level. There was little disagreement to the notion that the future of wrestling could well be in the hands of women's wrestling. Bardis declared that besides returning wrestling to the Olympic program, perhaps this could be one of the strongest legacies that CPOW can bring to the United States for the sport of wrestling.

On the fundraising agenda, Bill Scherr noted that the monies raised to date by CPOW (approximately $1.3 million) appeared to be enough to cover expenses up through September 8 and the group would look to develop a focused fundraising plan after the Buenos Aires vote.

What no one discussed on this call was the potential financial consequences to organizations like FILA, CPOW, USA Wrestling and the other national wrestling federations, if, in a worse-case scenario, the IOC General Assembly did not vote wrestling back into the Olympic Games. No one wanted to seriously consider those potential 'evil times' facing the sport and its most senior organizations.

Lee Roy Smith took a few minutes to heap some laurels on CPOW's efforts during the campaign to save wrestling. Smith said: "CPOW did a great deal to help guide FILA. I was very impressed with CPOW's diverse leadership. It wasn't easy to guide such independent-minded people. I want to acknowledge one of the key decisions made by CPOW Chair Bill Scherr and his brother Jim was to keep us from attacking the IOC.

"Everything in my senses wanted to go after those that made the decision to put wrestling on the outside. It took a while for me to rationalize that we needed to guide FILA to accepting responsibility and demonstrating how a 'New FILA' will become a better partner for the IOC and the Olympic movement. Clearly the world sentiment was in our favor, yet we could not tactically make the IOC the culprit.

"I think we did a good job of activating more social media that could inform and inspire people with our message. The importance of strategic communications and messaging were keys to unifying the wrestling communities at home and abroad, and hopefully we can continue to unify all the entities in the USA around common messaging in the future."

During August, some in FILA were thinking ahead about potential adjustments to the new rules after the Senior World Championships in Budapest in September. Preliminary data from the World University Games and Junior World Championships indicated that there was a time savings per bout under the new rules vs prior year contests. That trend would have to be verified at the Senior World Championships. A proposal was floated seeking a survey in Budapest of coaches, wrestlers, researchers, and media to establish the priorities for using any time savings, should there be any.

The potential options...

- Increase the point difference from seven to 10 to earn a technical fall;
- Eliminate two three-point takedowns ending a match;
- Eliminate five-point grand amplitude throws ending a match;
- Increase the minimum rest time between bouts;
- Install overtime instead of criteria in case of ties;
- Change the repechage to include the losers to the semi-finalists;
- Do a combination of the above and reduce the period time to 2:30 per period;
- Make no changes; the wrestling time per day has reached the fan's capacity or tolerance.

Keeping the wrestling momentum moving along with another newsworthy event, organizers in Georgia planned a send-off for the USA Freestyle team on their way to the upcoming World championships with a Rally4Wrestling extravaganza over Labor Day weekend. Held at the Cooler, a popular sports complex in Alpharetta, Georgia owned by John Bardis, the three-day event featured appearances by an impressive group of wrestling heroes — Dan Gable, Bruce Baumgartner, John Smith, Tom Brands, Brandon Slay, Lee Kemp, Nate Carr, John Azevedo and Wade Schalles.

As the dog days came to a close, the British bookmakers posted their odds on the sport winning the IOC vote come September 8...

Wrestling 4:7
Squash 7:4
Baseball/softball 8:1

Nevertheless, no one in the worldwide wrestling family was taking anything for granted.

CHAPTER 24 / **Buenos Aires... Vote #3**

THE HILTON HOTEL, Buenos Aires was the eye of the Olympic storm during the 125th session of the IOC General Assembly from September 7-10, 2013. Local police had the area well cordoned off for several blocks on all sides. You needed special accreditation to even go near the hotel, and one rite of passage (say, a media pass) didn't allow one to go much further than the sectioned-off designated media area.

All of this so that the IOC general assembly could vote in relative peace on three deliberate matters...

• The host city for the 2020 Games
• The choice between baseball/softball, squash and wrestling as a 2020 and 2024 'provisional' Olympic sport
• The election of a new IOC President

The vote for the 'sport to be added' was sandwiched between the other two issues. The host city vote was scheduled for Saturday, September 7; the vote for the new President would be held on Tuesday, the final day of the session. Sunday morning was reserved for wrestling and its two competitors.

FILA President Lalovic and most of his presentation team and consultants arrived in Buenos Aires more than a week before the actual presentation day. They had preparatory work that needed to be accomplished — putting the finishing touches to the presentation and starting the rehearsal process. They were staying in the expansive Sheraton Hotel — on the same floor as their competing baseball/softball and squash entourages.

One of the presenters, Daniel Igali, arrived a few days later than the rest of the contingent. He had caught malaria from a mosquito in late August and spent four days in the hospital in his native Nigeria. Knowing his importance to the Olympic vote, the doctors and officials there treated him with extra care and had him on the mend and off to Argentina just a week after contacting the disease.

Almost immediately upon arrival in Buenos Aires, Lalovic had to deal with an emerging problem. He learned through his own sources that the Japan Wrestling Federation had recently sent a letter asking for support of wrestling's Olympic bid to the 177 wrestling federations — and, unfortunately, it had also gone to some IOC members. The IOC's Rules of Conduct prohibits communications of this type during the last three weeks before the vote between the bidding sports and IOC members.

What to do? Really, there was just one option — FILA had to turn itself in to the IOC and take the consequences.

Lalovic informed the IOC of FILA's error along with a sincere apology. On Friday, August 30 the IOC sent their official warning to wrestling's international federation. Several days later, on September 3, FILA received a confirmation letter from the IOC's Chris Dubi stating that they, and the Japan Federation, had received a reprimand for engaging in activities not in line with the IOC's rules. The IOC stated that they now considered the matter closed.

The IOC copied the letter to the baseball/softball and squash federation presidents.

There was no mention of this incident in any of the IOC, FILA or any other media releases, until Friday, September 6, the morning of FILA's only scheduled press conference before the Sunday vote. The website Around the Rings broke the story with the glaring headline, 'IOC Reprimands Wrestling Federation'. The site had obtained a copy of the September 3 letter.

When Around the Rings received the letter, and from whom, was not disclosed. It was sure to be a hot topic at the noon press conference.

Bob Condron served as host at the press briefing, attended by scores of correspondents and photographers in the Hilton hotel media wing. He introduced from the dais members of the Sunday presentation team — Carol Huynh, Lise Legrand, Daniel Igali, Jim Scherr, Each spoke a few, actually very few, words about the new direction of wrestling since February 12 or in the case of Legrand and Igali, the importance of their experience as a wrestler.

When it was Condron's time to introduce Lalovic, he asked the FILA president to speak a little about the journey wrestling had taken since February and to comment on "a letter he just received". Lalovic spent the next five minutes or so going over the changes wrestling has made. "Having traveled through troubled waters, we can now see the harbor," he remarked.

It was then question-and-answer time; naturally, the first question from one of the press corps was, "What about the letter of reprimand that FILA have received from the IOC?"

There was a slight gasp — not everyone in the room was aware of the matter.

Lalovic was forthright in handling the question — and the others that followed. He explained that the Japanese group had made an honest mistake in trying to influence IOC members after a moratorium deadline and FILA informed the IOC of the error. He considered the issue closed.

Moving beyond the inquiries about the reprimand, panel members answered questions about "the surprise" of the February IOC recommendation (Carol Huynh called it "the best worst-thing to happen to wrestling") and Jim Scherr addressed the new emphasis on better and broader television coverage of wrestling in the 2016 Games. Lalovic and Condron passed out a handful of the new brochures describing the new World Plan for Wrestling.

Lalovic concluded the session with an anecdote about the growing popularity of wrestling worldwide, citing a recent wrestling event in Switzerland. The week-long festival in this tiny country, not noted for wrestling prowess, drew 300,000 spectators in total — 50,000 for the finals alone. A remarkable show of interest for 'new wrestling'!

Still, as one left the media center, the vision of IOC members reading Friday's Around the Rings headline sent mild, but unneeded, tremors to the hearts of more than a few wrestling supporters.

Saturday brought rain, rain and more rain to the Argentinian capital as the 125th International Olympic Committee session officially opened. Figuratively, it really rained on Istanbul's and Madrid's parade. The IOC voters awarded the 2020 Games to Tokyo, Japan, which ran away with the election. Madrid was eliminated first, and Tokyo garnered 60 votes to Istanbul's 36 in the decisive round of voting.

There was a tale about the fate of Madrid's bid making the rounds of the cocktail-hour circuit after the vote. Had Juan Samaranch Jr.'s efforts to sway the IOC Executive Board to oust wrestling in lieu of modern pentathlon cost Madrid its bid to host the 2020 Olympic Games? It seems as though numerous IOC members were not pleased with the Executive Board's recommendation in February to eliminate wrestling. Voting wrestling back at this point, as most wanted to do, would appear to some as a condemnation for the IOC process; it would not serve the original purpose of adding a 'new' sport.

Though no one would confirm it, perhaps voters crossed Spain off their ballot in a retaliatory measure against Samaranch. It was rumored that General Assembly members intimated to colleagues that to preserve the reputation of the IOC,

Lise Legrand and Carol Huynh appear relaxed as they await a press conference two days before the critical IOC vote.

they could not vote for Madrid, otherwise they'd look like a cozy country club for the sake of Samaranch's modern pentathlon. Poetic justice?

Interestingly, only 96 IOC members voted on Saturday out of a possible 103 in the General Assembly. Presumably, some members were unable to attend the session.

Wrestling's presentation team spent Saturday cornered in the Sheraton, rehearsing some more and trying to get a decent pre-game-day rest. It was not much different than the day before wrestling in the NCAA (or Olympic) finals — except no one was concerned with making weight.

Huynh and Igali reflected on their task as presenters. Huynh commented, "It's been terrific to have the chance to give back to the sport that I love. I have really enjoyed working with Mr. Lalovic. He's been doing some amazing things with FILA and hopefully he'll continue. He's been a great leader of our team."

Igali pitched in with some high praise for the consultants: "The people at

Teneo have been awesome. They are true professionals who helped us so much with our presentation. They have become like family. We started working with them well before the St. Petersburg presentations, first by phone and emails and then in person. They put us at ease. It was not just any one person — everyone we worked with there was fabulous."

A couple of wrestling leaders from the U.S, Dziedzic and Bill Scherr, were in a positive mood about the next day's vote. They believed that the General Assembly would ratify the February 12 Executive Board recommendation on the 25 core sports going forward. They dared to think out loud about winning the vote against baseball/softball and squash. That would bring wrestling back as a 'provisional' sport. The question is the air — What would wrestling need to do to become a core sport once again?

Dziedzic and Scherr came to the same conclusion — that an answer to that question probably couldn't be answered precisely until after the vote for the new IOC President, scheduled for Tuesday. One of the favored candidates for the position, Germany's Thomas Bach, had hinted that the cap on 25 core sports could be adjusted, with more emphasis placed on controlling the number of total athletes than the number of sports. There was speculation that one of the other two sports vying for 'provisional' status could be added as early as the Sochi IOC session in 2014.

They both agreed that as opposed to the Martinetti regime, FILA and the national federations would be constantly listening and watching for signals from the new IOC President and reacting accordingly. And the work to continually improve the sport starts again next week.

Sunday morning in Buenos Aires was glorious. The dark storm clouds had moved on; the air was crisp, the skies clear, with the brilliant spring sunshine inviting all to enjoy nature's gift of fine weather.

The much anticipated sport selection session started at 9am Buenos Aires time (one hour ahead of EST). The schedule called for three hours of discussions and presentations. The final vote was expected to take place at high noon. The session would be broadcast live via the website all morning around the world. To the devout in America, this likely meant missing their Sunday morning church service — though prayers were surely being relayed upstairs by many.

The first hour was rather perfunctory. There was a recitation on the history of how the IOC got to today's vote, starting with the July, 2011 decision to identify eight sports for possible inclusion as 'new' sports for 2020 and 2024. At the time baseball and softball were separate federations and both were on the 2011 list.

One of the General Assembly members, Canadian Dick Pound, caused a gentle stir when he tried to make a motion to postpone today's voting another five months to give the Executive Board a second chance to drop a sport besides the ancient Olympic staple of wrestling. President Rogge gracefully rejected the request, saying, "We should act now."

At 10:05 Christophe De Kepper, IOC Director General, called for the first vote of the session — to ratify the Executive Board's recommendation of the 25 core sports for the 2020 and 2024 Games. President Rogge indicated that he would not participate in the vote, which was conducted electronically by secret ballot. Within three minutes the vote opened, closed and was tabulated. The General Assembly voted to ratify the recommended 25 core sports by a landslide 77-16 margin, with two abstains. No surprise there.

Officially, for the first time in the history of the modern Games, wrestling was no longer a core Olympic sport.

It was time for the three presentations. Baseball/softball led off, pleading its case to return to the program. In 2005, baseball and softball were individually voted out of the Games, becoming the first sports expelled since polo was dropped from the 1936 Olympics. The presenters stressed the popularity of the two sports, the gender equality aspect of combining the two federations, and the availability of generous sponsorships. The legendary Don Porter, co-president of the baseball/softball federation, made an emotional and personal case for his beloved sports at the close of the presentation.

After a 25-minute break, it was squash's turn to convince the assembly that they were the most worthy of the one open spot on the Olympic program. Squash emphasized it was a sport of the future, not the past, and featured videos of athletes playing on state-of-the-art transportable glass-walled courts. They played the youth card with their presentation team, which included 25-year old world champion Ramy Ashour followed by two teenagers selling their love for the game.

Wrestling's moment had come. At 11:36am Nenad Lalovic led his team to the presenter's platform.

Lalovic, the 'diamond in the rough who turned into a diamond' as John Bardis once described him, proudly led off his team's remarks announcing that, "Today is the most important day in the 3,000-year history of wrestling. Today's vote is crucial for wrestling's survival. This is the greatest competition of our life." He spoke for the next four minutes about the many changes that wrestling had made since February that transformed FILA back into the Olympic family.

Jim Scherr, who moved to Baku, Azerbaijan with his family three months before and who never seemed to get enough recognition due him during the campaign, spoke next. Scherr pointed out, "Wrestling is new in every way" and that the 'new wrestling' has invigorated its competitors and fans to new heights in the last few months.

A short video showing action-packed wrestling scenes came next, followed by Lise Legrand's turn at the microphone. The Olympic and world medalist from France spoke eloquently for two minutes in her native French, telling the assembly of how her experiences as a female wrestler has enriched her life and career. Daniel Igali and Carol Huynh followed, each using their St. Petersburg presentation as the base for their talk, Igali expanding a bit as he spoke of how "wrestling has transformed me and now wrestling is transforming itself."

Huynh, who will be honored as a new inductee into the FILA Hall of Fame later in September, shouldered the responsibility of being the last presenter of wrestling's case to the members. She captured her audience with her wrap-up: "I recently retired from competition and I coach athletes working hard to make National teams and future Olympic Games. These kids eat, sleep and breathe wrestling. They would be devastated if our sport is not on the Olympic program.

"So, in a very real sense I'm here today for them as an Olympian and a part of history and a role model for young people. I want these future generations of young wrestlers to believe that they can make history, too. That is why we spent the last six months transforming our sport, dear members. We created a 'new wrestling' on behalf of our sport."

Following another short video, Lalovic closed out the presentation. It was time for questions and answers. The other two sports had received one or two obligatory questions. Not so with wrestling.

The first question from the assembly floor dealt with allegations of "corruption" within the wrestling ranks. Now if that didn't smell like a plant...

Six other questions followed — some direct, such as, "How many athletes and how many events will there be in the 'new wrestling?'" and, "What about Greco-Roman competition for women?" Some were more obscure, such as, "What about the mistakes wrestling has made?"

It was evident that the team was well prepared to answer any question thrown at them, and yet there was a bit of a mood shift. The 20-minute presentation and video was very upbeat. Feedback from many quarters over the last month had been upbeat. Suddenly, it felt like some in the assembly were determined to pick at a scab. As Lalovic eased his way around the "corruption" issue — which was more of a garbled statement than a question from the floor — and his admission of numerous mistakes in the past, the negativity was starting to feel awkward for some. Huynh helped things by expertly handling the women's Greco issue, and Scherr spoke clearly about the new 6-6-6 format with approximately 340 competitors. Time was up and the team departed the room.

It was 12:18pm — time to go to the vote.

De Kepper again presided over the voting and once again President Rogge announced that he had elected not to cast a ballot. The 95 General Assembly members present (one less than the previous day) were instructed to tap #5 on the electronic machine to vote for baseball/softball; tap #6 for squash; tap #8 for wrestling. Those numbers were drawn randomly just moments earlier by selected IOC voting members.

The winning sport needed to receive a simple majority of the 95 votes — at least 48. If no sport received that many, the sport with the least number of votes in that first round would be eliminated and there would be a runoff in a second round.

At 12:25pm De Kepper announced that the voting was now open. Two minutes later he closed the vote.

Moments later a small group of assigned IOC members examined the electronic results. Without emotion they showed the results to Rogge and went through the exercise of signing the tally. Rogge announced, "Bring the federations back into the room." The immediate speculation was that one of the sports had won a majority on the first ballot.

First the baseball/softball group entered the large hall and took their seats in the front row. Squash followed, taking second-row seats. The wrestling group, including the presenters and key leaders from around the world, jostled their way into the third row. Hearts were thumping. After 208 days of sweat and toil, this was it.

At 12:32pm Buenos Aires time, IOC president Rogge stood at the podium and decreed, "With 49 votes, wrestling has been elected for the 2020 Games."

The thrill of victory; the agony of defeat. The wrestling delegation react after the Buenos Aires vote.
Fabrice Coffrini/AFP/Getty